101
EPIC
DISHES

Recipes That Teach You
How to Make the Classics
Even More Delicious

JET **TILA** ALI **TILA**

Award-Winning Chef and TV Personality   Culinary Educator

PAGE STREET
PUBLISHING CO.

PAGE STREET
PUBLISHING CO.

This book is dedicated to Chef Tad Weyland Fukumoto.
You've been our business partner, family, collaborator and partner in crime for over 20 years.
Thank you, brother! #TeamTila for life!

CONTENTS

FOREWORD BY BOBBY FLAY

Jet Tila is one of the most interesting and dynamic people I have met in the food business. His experience is as vast as his personality and it all stems from one place—the stove!

I've eaten his food when he was the chef of a contemporary Asian restaurant in Las Vegas and I've watched him battle on *Beat Bobby Flay*, where he had a bowl of his famous Drunken Noodles in his back pocket ready to take me on, but my favorite moments with Jet are when neither of us are cooking. Oh, don't worry—we're eating—it's just that someone else is making it happen in the kitchen. It usually revolves around an amazing hole-in-the-wall restaurant somewhere in Thai Town in Los Angeles. Jet is the guy to know when you're salivating for the spicy, sweet, sour flavors of Thailand . . . real Thai food that will light you up like a Christmas tree if you don't have the guidance of Mr. Tila.

I spend a lot of time watching Jet demonstrate his wares on TV and every social media platform ever invented. Watch carefully . . . He's incredibly likeable and very endearing, but his most effective weapon is his knowledge of cooking. And not just in Thai cuisine and some of the other Asian cuisines he somehow managed to master. He's serious about what he does but presents it in the most friendly and accessible way possible. Jet's been able to combine two skills that most people have attempted but have come up short: He's able to combine his chops as a professional chef and fold them into a likeable but authoritative personality that everyone, it seems, wants a piece of.

I consider Jet a really good friend beyond our common passion for cooking. When my daughter, Sophie, abandoned the East Coast for college at the University of Southern California a few years back, it was Jet who gave this father some much needed confidence that his daughter would be safe on her own in L.A. He said one simple thing to me that resonated throughout my body as a permanent stamp of his friendship and loyalty: "Bobby, I want you to know that if anything goes down with Sophie while she's in L.A., I've got you covered." It was one sentence and it was shorthand for I'll do whatever I have to if she needs my help in any circumstance, and I believed every breath of it.

Jet and I have similar stories: two American kids who needed to work with their hands before we could find true inspiration in our lives. We both found it in the kitchen. We spent a little more time than we probably should have out of the classroom but somehow our experiences in the places we shouldn't have been helped shape our work ethics so we were able to succeed, and taught us how to navigate through the unexpected. That's how I knew that Sophie would be fine under Jet's watchful eye from a distance.

Speaking of the unexpected, this new cookbook from Jet Tila is not a solo album. This go-around, Jet is teaming up with his lovely and creative wife, Ali. This book is not about the Asian cuisine that we're so used to hearing Jet expound about, but true American classics that we all crave over and over. It's from the Tila family's home kitchen.

Just rifling through this book makes me fold over pages of recipes that will certainly inspire me on many Sunday nights in the future. I'll be giving Low and Slow Prime Rib Roast with Horseradish Cream (page 28) or Sunday Night Chicken Parmesan (page 49) and Roasted Cauliflower Steak with Agrodolce, Golden Raisins and Pine Nuts (page 135) and of course the Da Bomb Budino: Italian Salted Caramel Pudding (page 187) a spin in my home kitchen for sure. I know the recipes will work perfectly because Jet says so. I treat this book as I do Jet and Ali Tila . . . as trusted friends.

—BOBBY FLAY, NYC

INTRODUCTION

Let's be real. It's hard to try to distill the world of food down into 101 recipes. Are we expecting to teach you how to cook everything? Well, no, but we sure can teach you how to take your cooking up many levels! We will really get down to the techniques that are key and hit many of the dishes that all good cooks should know. We're not going to try to teach you everything; instead, we'll teach you the most important things. Cooking takes thousands of hours to master, and we want to practice the recipes that are key to becoming great. I will be your Mr. Miyagi, young Daniel's master instructor in *The Karate Kid*! You'll be waxing on and waxing off, you will be sanding the floor and painting the fence. And soon you'll realize that with each meal you were learning what you needed to get you good and fast! And we'll make it as easy as possible.

So, basically, we wrote this book because we want to make you a better cook! We think that the difference between a good cook and a great cook is understanding the *why*, not just the *how*. Our goal for this book is to take you deeper into the *why* of cooking, and to show you how chefs approach recipes and give dishes that little extra something. Chefs have secrets to seasoning and plating, and maybe we'll even show you a way to do something you've never seen or imagined. We want to open the door to some of these tips and secrets.

Each recipe will teach you at least one key culinary technique similar to something taught in culinary school. That means you will have learned 101 new techniques by the time you cook through this book.

There's a cumulative learning effect to cooking and practicing these recipes. For instance, learning how to cook a perfect steak is really a lot of small lessons in one. You learn what internal temperatures equate to particular doneness levels. You learn about searing. You learn about seasoning. And all of those rules don't just apply to steak. Then you make mashed potatoes. That will teach you about cooking potatoes until they are buttery, which will apply to other potato or root vegetable recipes. Then you'll learn how to roast Brussels sprouts, which teaches a great lesson about roasting in general. Between those three dishes, you've just cooked the perfect dinner. But guess what? You've also learned multiple techniques that will apply to dozens of dishes. It's like building a house with bricks, but what's cool is that each recipe isn't just one brick—it's like ten. And the more you cook, the faster and more accurate you get.

Each recipe has an introduction that prepares you and gives you some information about the dish. We lay out the ingredients in the order they are used. The more you cook, the more you'll start to see the patterns of ingredients in the recipes. They are usually grouped in a certain order. Oil, garlic and aromatics usually go together. Proteins are usually prepped, patted dry and seasoned. Vegetables are cut certain ways for certain preparations. You will start to look at recipes like formulas, intuitively knowing when to add certain things to the pan or grill according to their group, also making you faster and more accurate. This helps you cook by feel and you'll be comfortable making substitutions.

We also add a "Chef Tip" here and there throughout the recipes. These tips help with certain ingredients or additional techniques, and you can apply them to other dishes with similar ingredients and techniques.

We usually place a dish into a category of cooking because it helps give you context. For example, a particular dish might be roasting, which is in the dry heat category. The oven temperature is set to 400°F (200°C), and eventually, it will be intuitive that roasting means: use the oven, set to 400°F (200°C); it's dry heat.

Most of these recipes are based on popular or classic dishes, the important dishes all cooks should have in their repertoire. But they have a twist that makes them special. Read through the book, cook the recipes a few times through and you will find your skills improve and your knowledge of food grow exponentially. You'll become more intuitive, faster and you'll really start enjoying yourself in the kitchen. Thomas Keller, award-winning chef and restaurateur, said, "Once you understand the foundations of cooking—whatever kind you like, whether it's French or Italian or Japanese—you really don't need a cookbook anymore." So here's to one of the last cookbooks you'll ever need!

THE FUNDAMENTALS OF GREAT COOKING

Here are the Tila cooking tenets, our dogma. These are the principles that we believe will make you a better cook and create more flavorful food. You might not understand them all yet, but you will by the end of this book!

1. Taste your food.

For some reason, a lot of cooks just don't taste their food enough! The easiest way to make any cook better is to reinforce this simple fundamental practice. Taste often as you're cooking, not just at the end to see whether it needs more seasoning (see #2). The more you taste, the more you teach your palate how flavors change throughout the cooking process. Remember to taste every step of a recipe. For instance, in a salad, taste the greens, the dressing and the final dish once tossed together.

2. Season everything well.

Season every layer and season as you go. Switch to kosher salt as your primary salt (see page 13 for more on this). The more you season with it, the more you realize food needs more salt than you think. It's almost impossible to overseason meat, and you have to season every component of a dish separately. This is the most important factor to making a delicious dish, so take your time and be sure to season and taste often (remember #1 above). Tasting and seasoning go together.

3. Brown food tastes good.

That means caramelization, char and browning always make your food taste better. Browning in food is called the Maillard reaction, which is a reaction of the amino acids and sugars in food when dry heat is applied. From bread and meat to vegetables, browning is key to flavor. Browning also evaporates moisture in food, which concentrates flavor. Obviously, browning too long will burn food and burned is usually bad, but a little bit of char in large portions can add a lot of flavor.

4. Mise en place.

This is French for "everything in its place," a fundamental concept in the kitchen, and it means so many things. It means get all your prep work done and organized before cooking. If everything is organized and ready, you limit the mistakes you can make. Cooking takes a balance of timing and managing multiple sense inputs all at once. Having your food, equipment and station organized helps you become proficient and efficient.

5. Understand dry and moist heat cooking.

All dishes fall into one category or the other, or use a combination of the two. Moist heat makes tough meats tender, but it cannot brown. Common examples of moist heat are steaming, boiling and poaching. It's great for breaking down foods to make them tender or rich, but alone it doesn't help with flavor. Dry heat makes things crispy and brown. Common examples are frying, sautéing, grilling and roasting. Dry heat will char, sear and intensify flavors. The combination of both categories is magical. Searing meat before you braise or boil it gives both flavor and tenderness.

6. Get to know your cut of meat.

Start to learn and pay attention to which muscles you are eating. You'll soon learn that muscles that do a lot of work—like chicken legs and thighs, chuck, short ribs and brisket—are tough but have more intense flavors. They usually take longer to cook to get them tender. Less frequently used muscles—like chicken breast, pork loin and filet mignon—are more tender. Tender meats cook quickly but are less flavorful.

7. Don't memorize recipes.

Instead, memorize the technique from each recipe you try. Recipes help you learn techniques. For example, let's say you're making stock. Once you remember the technique of making chicken stock, you can make beef stock, vegetable stock and even seafood stock. When you learn how to braise, you can braise anything, from short ribs to carnitas.

8. Practice makes great food.

Repetition is the key to making good cooks into great ones. Every chef has made the same dish thousands of times. There's also the belief that it takes 10,000 hours to become an expert at anything. Cooking a dish so many times that it becomes second nature makes you faster, more proficient and helps you learn tricks and tips.

THE TILA KITCHEN MUST-HAVES

We've compiled a list of our must-have kitchen items that we could not live without. They are either gadgets, tools or ingredients that we find ourselves using every day in the kitchen. We hope they make your cooking life easier and you find them as valuable as we do.

Pan spray (aka Pam aka pan release aka can of compressed oil)

This is our favorite kitchen item! So much so, we get made fun of by Team Tila all the time. We use it for sautéing, for baking, to get a better brown and to help parchment paper stick to pans. It's an amazing 6 calories per every second of spray and covers very evenly.

Side towels

We use two types of towels in the Tila house. First are bar mops. These are those white towels, sometimes with a colored stripe on them. Every commercial kitchen uses them for wiping down your station and equipment, sanitizing and grabbing hot pans. You can never have too many of them, but it's important to manage them and not cross-contaminate. We love the ones with a colored stripe down the middle because you can quickly differentiate between a side towel and a cleaning towel. We use side towels to cook with and microfiber to clean with, so we never cross-contaminate them.

Stand mixer

We love the KitchenAid mixers; in fact, we own four different ones, from 3- to 8-quart (2.7- to 7.2-L) models. Most cooks will be fine with a 4- to 5-quart (3.6- to 4.5-L) model. From mixing doughs and batters to whipping cream and meringues—there is no single appliance that can do this many jobs. You don't have to buy the Ferrari of mixers; something basic with a dough hook, a whip and a paddle is fine.

Enameled Dutch oven

If you were to own one piece of cookware that could do everything, this would be it. An enameled Dutch oven can deep-fry, sauté, braise, bake, boil and steam. We recommend at least a 7-quart (6.3-L) oven to have the room to do to what you need. They are pricey, but if you bought all the pans you needed for all the cooking methods mentioned above, it would cost way more than one great enameled cast-iron pot.

Mini prep food processor

This smaller food processor is perfect for smaller amounts of chopping prep or emulsifying dressings. It keeps you from pulling out the heavy giant for normal amounts of food prep. Again, no need to go crazy. We like the two-button, two-speed model with a single blade.

Sanitizer

We always keep a spray bottle of bleach and water sanitizer around. Commercial kitchens use chemical sanitizer in buckets, but this will work for the home. Sometimes you want to do a quick wipe-down of your cutting boards, countertops or tools. This is perfect for that.

Cooking scale

Whether you cook, bake or do both, you need a scale! Most bakers around the world weigh instead of measure volumes. The science of baking requires accuracy, and you can't wing it. Plus, if you find yourself cooking for large parties or starting to cater, the best way to multiply a recipe is by weight. Buy a cooking scale that shows both grams and ounces and can hold up to 11 pounds (5 kg) or more.

Thermometers

You need at least two thermometers. One should be digital instant read, the kind that has an arm that swings out 180 degrees. It should be waterproof, have a range of at least -60 to 500°F (-51 to 260°C) and have a large screen. This one is primarily to take meat temperatures, but it works for baking as well. The second should be an oven thermometer because you'd be surprised by how inaccurate home ovens are. In addition, you might have different temperatures in your oven based on where the rack is, so the thermometer will make sure you're at the right temperature every time.

Salts

We primarily use two salts in our house. Kosher salt is our all-purpose salt, and we use it for almost everything. We use Diamond Crystal brand for kosher salt. We are not sponsored—it's just the brand we love. The crystals are less dense and are easy to crush between the fingers and distribute evenly. For finishing salt, or what we call fancy salt, we love Maldon salt. It's flaky and flat and has a pleasant, salty ocean flavor.

KNIFE SKILLS AND TECHNIQUES THAT YOU WILL USE FOR ANY TYPE OF COOKING

Good knife skills are one of the most important aspects of being a great cook. Even, consistent cuts cook in the same amount of time and make a dish look beautiful. Having fast, accurate knife skills also cuts down on prep time. You spend a lot of your life cutting and chopping, so make it count. Here is some basic information, as well as a few tips, to help you up your knife work game.

Knife and cutting board selection

There are dozens and dozens of types of knives, and don't get us started on finishes and designs. It can be really confusing to choose a knife, but we'll keep it simple. In our opinion, you need to start with two basic knife types. You need a 6- to 8-inch (15- to 20-cm) chef's knife for most of your cutting work and an 8- to 9-inch (20- to 23-cm) serrated slicer to cut soft items like tomatoes and bread. These two knives will do 90 percent of all cutting tasks. Once you are comfortable with them, then you can move on to others and find your style of knife. Don't jump right in to a fancy expensive brand, because your preferences will change as you become more proficient. We also suggest investing a few bucks in a cut-resistant glove for your nondominant hand. You never cut your knife hand, so protect your other hand with a snug cut-resistant glove!

We love using wooden boards, specifically walnut, maple or cherry. They are firm enough for slicing and chopping but soft enough to absorb the everyday pounding and won't dull your knives too quickly. They do require some oiling and conditioning but will stay beautiful for decades! Commercial-grade high-density boards are also great and easier to maintain than wood. Look for the NSF logo on commercial plastic boards, which means they meet national health and safety standards.

Knife grip

Let's break down the chef's knife into its parts. The handle is below the blade and where you place your hand. The correct grip is to pinch the blade with your index and thumb and wrap your three remaining fingers around the handle. This grip helps the knife become an extension of your hand and gives you a rock-solid grip. Always anchor the food with your nondominant hand, making sure to always keep your thumb behind your four front fingers. Slicing is always in a down and forward direction, never just downward.

Primary cuts

French formal training has created names for almost all knife cuts. It's important to learn those names so you can talk like a chef. Speaking the same language in the kitchen makes for efficient work and you sound cool to non-cooks! The bulk of all cuts will either fall into a slice or a dice. Slice means something long and thin like a matchstick (julienne) or French fry (batonnet). Dice (aka chop) is always a box shape with specific measurements. A lot of recipes just say chopped or diced without a measurement; the default chop/dice is always ¼ inch (6 mm). What's left is rough chop and mince. Rough chop usually means cut larger than large dice with no specific shape. Mince is the opposite, meaning smaller than a small dice with no specific shape.

Dice

Large dice: ¾-inch (2-cm) cube
Medium dice: ½-inch (1.3-cm) cube
Small dice: ¼-inch (0.6-cm) cube
Brunoise: $\frac{1}{8}$-inch (0.3-cm) cube

Slice

Batonnet (thick slice): ¼ x ¼ x 2–3 inches (0.6 x 0.6 x 5–7.5 cm)
Julienne: $\frac{1}{8}$ x $\frac{1}{8}$ x 2–3 inches (0.3 x 0.3 x 5–7.5 cm)
Thin slice: ¼ inch (0.6 cm) wide x the length of the vegetable

Other Cuts

Mince: Evenly cut to smaller than small dice with no specific shape
Rough Chop: Evenly cut larger than large dice with no specific shape
Chiffonade: Lay leafy herbs over each other, roll, then slice into $\frac{1}{8}$-inch (0.3-cm) super-thin strips
Lyonnaise: Cut ¼-inch (0.6-cm) half-moon slices of onion with the grain

Common Yields

Here are some useful yields to make your cooking faster and easier. Commit these to memory as you cook.

1 Onion

Small (about 4 oz [112 g]): Yields ½ cup chopped
Medium (about 8 oz [224 g]): Yields 1 cup chopped
Large (about 12 oz [340 g]): Yields 1½ cups chopped

1 Medium Carrot (about 2 oz [56 g])

Yields ⅜ cup shredded or matchsticks
Yields ½ cup sliced
Yields ½ cup chopped

1 Celery Stalk (about 2 oz [56 g])

Yields ½ cup chopped
Yields ½ cup sliced

1 Large Bell Pepper (about 5 oz [142 g])

Yields 1¼ cups sliced
Yields 1 cup chopped

Citrus

1 lemon (about 4 oz [112 g]): Yields 3 tablespoons (45 ml) juice and 1 tablespoon (6 g) zest
1 lime (about 3 oz [84 g]): Yields 2 tablespoons (30 ml) juice and 2 teaspoons (4 g) zest
1 orange (about 8 oz [224 g]): Yields ⅓ cup (80 ml) juice and 2 tablespoons (12 g) zest

BEEF

The Low-Down on Cooking Restaurant-Quality Beef Dishes Perfectly Every Time

Beef is not just what's for dinner. It's a riddle, wrapped in a mystery, inside an enigma. But we are gonna figure it out together! As with most four-legged animals that we consume, each area of the cow needs its own special heat and technique. In this chapter, we'll walk you through the basic cuts and incredible recipes you can make to draw out the most flavor from each part of the cow.

The mid-back, or rib area, is where all the steaks we love to eat come from. Those muscles don't move much, so they stay relatively tender. The rule of thumb is dry heat and quick cooking are best for tender cuts. Learn to create the perfect steak with a delicious golden crust in a cast-iron skillet with my recipe on page 18. I'll also show you how to make perfect prime rib on page 28.

Moist, long cooks like braising and stewing are best for tougher cuts, such as short ribs, shank and brisket. These parts of the animal move a lot, so the muscle is much firmer. Tougher cuts have more flavor but need to be tortured into tenderness to be delicious. You'll learn all the details when you master my French-Style Oven-Braised Brisket with Red Wine Onions (page 19). We'll also make a rich Irish stew (page 21).

Another way to make beefy tough cuts instantly tender and be able to cook with quick dry heat is to grind them into burgers, meatballs or kabobs. Great burgers are ground blends of different muscle groups that create beefy deliciousness.

Beef Doneness Temperatures
Rare (before resting): 115°F (46°C)
Medium-rare (before resting): 120 to 130°F (49 to 54°C)
Medium (before resting): 140°F (60°C)
Medium-well (before resting): 150°F (66°C)
Well-done (before resting): 155 to 160°F (68 to 71°C)
Ground beef: Only apply the above temperatures to whole muscle from trusted sources. If buying store-made ground beef blends, cook to 160 to 165°F (71 to 74°C) always!

Perfect Pan-Roasted Rib-Eye Steak

Some keys to cooking the perfect pan steak are getting a deep brown crust and finishing in the oven. A cast-iron skillet is essential for this because of its ability to hold heat and go from stove to oven. My secret is dusting steak with sugar because it caramelizes and helps get that deep brown bark. The sweetness also pairs beautifully with the savory steak. I love rib eye because of its balance between fat and lean with nice gristle bits. Ali prefers a leaner, more tender cut like filet. In the pan, the same rules apply as long as the thickness and weights are similar.

Serves 2-4

2 tsp (12 g) kosher salt

½ tsp ground black pepper

2 tsp (8 g) sugar

2 (12–16-oz [340–454-g]) rib-eye steaks, 1" (2.5 cm) thick

2 tsp (10 ml) grapeseed or vegetable oil

4 tbsp (56 g) butter

2 cloves garlic, smashed but left whole

4–6 sprigs thyme

2 sprigs rosemary

In a small bowl, combine the kosher salt, pepper and sugar. Season both steaks evenly and generously. Knock off any excess seasoning. Store the steaks in the fridge, uncovered, overnight.

Allow the steaks to come to room temperature for an hour and pat dry with paper towels prior to cooking.

Preheat the oven to 400°F (200°C). Preheat a 10- to 12-inch (25- to 30-cm) cast-iron skillet over high heat, about 450°F (230°C).

Add the oil to the pan. Sear the steaks in the pan for about 2 minutes, undisturbed, until a deep golden brown crust forms. Turn over to sear the second side until golden brown, for an additional minute. Add the butter, garlic and herbs. Swirl until the butter melts. Baste the melted butter and herbs over the steaks 6 to 8 times, until the steaks are coated well. Place the pan into the oven to finish.

For medium-rare, cook for 4 minutes, or until the internal temperature reaches 125°F (52°C). Remove from the oven, cover loosely with foil and rest for 5 minutes. Serve whole or slice thin and fan onto a plate. Drizzle the pan butter and herbs on before serving.

Chef Tip: The secret to getting a deep brown crust on a steak is to make sure the surface is as dry as possible. Don't believe the old wives' tale that preseasoning will dry out your steaks. In fact, we encourage you to season and store in the fridge for 24 to 48 hours before cooking. That will dry out just the exterior, which will make a gorgeous crust.

French-Style Oven-Braised Brisket with Red Wine Onions

Brisket comes from the lower chest of the cow and is a very strong muscle, which means it has a lot of beefy flavor and takes time to cook down. The essential technique here is braising, which will make any tough cut yield into a tender, luscious experience. Be sure to brown well and use a heavy enameled Dutch oven. Make this instead of pot roast and you'll have your guests wanting the recipe! As with all braises, serving a day or two later is actually better.

Serves 4

Brisket

4–5-lb (1.8–2.3-kg) first or flat cut brisket

Salt and ground pepper, to taste

2 tbsp (30 ml) olive oil

1½ cups (240 g) chopped yellow onion

½ cup (60 g) diced carrot

2 cloves garlic, finely chopped

1 (28-oz [784-g]) can plum (Roma) tomatoes, with juices

1 cup (235 ml) Merlot or other full-bodied red wine

2 bay leaves

Red Wine Onions

2 tbsp (30 ml) olive oil

3 cups (480 g) thinly sliced sweet onion, such as Vidalia

Salt and ground pepper, to taste

1 cup (235 ml) Merlot or other full-bodied red wine

½ cup (80 g) pitted dried cherries, divided

Preheat the oven to 325°F (170°C).

To make the brisket, season the meat on all sides with salt and pepper. In a Dutch oven or a large, wide ovenproof pan with a tight-fitting lid, warm the olive oil over medium-high heat. Add the brisket and brown well on both sides, about 6 minutes total. Transfer to a plate. Add the onion and carrot to the pan and sauté until golden, about 5 minutes. Add the garlic and sauté until softened, about 1 minute. Add the tomatoes and juices, wine and bay leaves. Mix well and bring to a boil. Return the brisket to the pan, cover and place in the oven.

Cook, basting occasionally with the pan juices, until fork tender, about 3 hours. Remove from the oven and let cool in the juices. Carefully lift the brisket from the juices and transfer to a deep platter. Cover with aluminum foil and refrigerate until cold, at least 2 hours or up to overnight. Let the pan juices cool, then pass through a food mill or press through a sieve into a bowl and set aside. Discard the solids.

Meanwhile, to make the onions, in a large frying pan, warm the olive oil over medium-low heat. Add the onions and sauté, stirring often, until golden brown, about 20 minutes. Season with salt and pepper. While the onions are cooking, pour the wine into a saucepan. Add ¼ cup (40 g) of the dried cherries and bring to a boil over high heat. Boil until reduced by half, about 5 minutes. Stir in the puréed brisket juices and return to a boil. Season to taste with salt and pepper.

Just before serving, preheat the oven to 350°F (180°C). Cut the brisket across the grain into thin slices. Arrange the slices, slightly overlapping, on an ovenproof serving platter. Cover with aluminum foil and place in the oven for 15 minutes to heat through.

To serve, remove the brisket from the oven. Pour the sauce evenly over the top. Top with the caramelized onions and the remaining ¼ cup (40 g) of dried cherries. Serve immediately.

> **Chef Tip:** The secret to caramelizing onions is low and slow. Slice your onions evenly and don't touch them once they are in the pan! It'll take time, but the onions will get brown and super sweet on their own.

Thick and Creamy Irish Beer Beef Stew

The classic definition of "stewing" is meat cooked in liquid long and slow until tender. The result usually ends in a thickened liquid. Some secrets to making great stew are using a beefy tough cut, like chuck, sirloin or brisket. We love using a combination at times. Dusting the beef cubes with flour helps remove moisture and aids in browning. Later the flour binds to the cooking liquid and creates a rich, creamy mouthfeel. Lastly, tomato purée is rich in glutamates (aka umami). We always add some to braises.

Serves 4

2 lb (910 g) sirloin tips or boneless beef chuck, trimmed and cut into 2" (5-cm) cubes

3 tbsp (45 ml) vegetable oil, divided

2 tbsp (16 g) all-purpose flour

1 tsp salt, or to taste

Freshly ground pepper, to taste

Pinch of cayenne

2 large onions, coarsely chopped

1 large clove garlic, crushed (optional)

2 tbsp (30 g) tomato purée

12 oz (355 ml) Guinness stout beer

1½ cups (355 ml) beef stock

12 oz (340 g) carrots, cut into large dice

12 oz (340 g) baby or red-skinned potatoes, cut into large dice

2 tsp (10 ml) soy sauce, or more to taste

2 sprigs thyme

½ tsp beef base (optional)

Chopped fresh parsley, for garnish

Preheat the oven to 300°F (150°C).

In a large bowl, toss the beef cubes with 1 tablespoon (15 ml) of the oil to coat. Add the flour, salt, freshly ground pepper and a pinch or two of cayenne. Toss the meat in the mixture until coated.

Heat the remaining 2 tablespoons (30 ml) of oil in a deep Dutch oven over high heat. Brown the meat for 1 minute on each side in three separate batches so you don't lose heat by crowding the pan. Add the onions, crushed garlic and tomato purée to the pan, cover and cook gently for about 5 minutes.

Deglaze the pan by pouring the Guinness into the Dutch oven and scraping up the caramelized brown bits with a spoon. Add the beef stock, bring to a boil and stir well. Add the carrots, potatoes, soy sauce, thyme and beef base (if using). Stir, taste and add a little more salt if necessary. Bring to a boil once again, then reduce to a simmer and cover with the lid of the casserole. Transfer to the oven and bake for about 3½ hours. Alternatively, simmer very gently on the stove until the meat is tender, 2½ to 3 hours.

Taste and correct the seasoning. Scatter with lots of chopped parsley.

> **Chef Tips:** The stout beer is perfect because it cooks down to add its dark chocolate and coffee notes, making a hearty classic stew.
>
> As with most soups and stews, it's even better the day after it's made.
>
> Other root veggies would also work well in this recipe, such as parsnips, turnips and rutabagas.

Keftas: My Fave Ground-Beef Kabobs with Lebneh Sauce

This is a Tila house favorite and one of the dishes Ali and I had on our first date. We also competed on *Guy's Grocery Games* making this dish and won best dish of that round, so don't pass this one by! A kabob is simply any meat or seafood cooked on a skewer or spit. It's a technique you need to know because of its limitless applications using a wide range of proteins. Another key technique is to grate your onions either with a food processor or box grater and use them as a paste. This really helps distribute the onion flavor throughout.

Serves 6

18 (6'' [15-cm]) wood skewers

Lebneh Sauce
1 cup (240 g) thick Greek yogurt
1 tbsp (15 ml) lemon juice
1 small clove garlic, minced
10 fresh mint leaves, finely chopped
1–2 tsp (6–12 g) kosher salt
1 tsp finely chopped fresh dill

Kabobs
1 medium yellow onion
5 cloves garlic
4 tbsp (15 g) finely chopped parsley
1 tsp ground sumac
2 tbsp (15 g) ground cumin
1 tsp ground coriander
1 tbsp (7 g) paprika
½ tsp ground cinnamon
1 tsp kosher salt
¼ tsp ground black pepper
2 tbsp (30 ml) extra virgin olive oil
2 lb (910 g) ground beef

Chef Tips: You can switch up the protein here. Chicken and lamb are great for this recipe. Also, you can cook them in a flat pan or even a griddle. So, don't let the lack of a grill deter you from making these delicious skewers.

Soak the skewers in warm water for at least 1 hour. This will keep them from burning.

Meanwhile, to make the lebneh sauce, in a small bowl, combine all of the lebneh ingredients. Taste and adjust the seasonings as needed. Chill in the fridge until ready to serve.

To make the kabobs, if you are preparing them by hand, grate the onion on the large holes of a box grater. Press out the excess liquid in a sieve. Smash the garlic, then mince finely, along with the parsley. In a large bowl, combine the onion, garlic, parsley, spices, oil and ground beef.

If you're using a food processor, rough chop the onion, then process to a rough paste. Scrape down the bowl and process again as needed. Transfer to a strainer and press to remove excess liquid. Return to the processor and add the garlic, parsley, spices and oil. Process until well combined. Transfer to a large bowl and add the ground beef.

With your hands, knead the beef with the seasonings until thoroughly combined. It may start out crumbly, but it should come together. Knead for 2 to 3 minutes, until the mixture is uniform and holds its shape. Divide into 18 golf ball–size portions, approximately 3 ounces (84 g) each. Lightly roll into a football shape, then flatten to approximately ½ inch (1.3 cm). Pierce with the skewer, place in a container, cover and hold in the refrigerator for at least 2 hours, which allows the flavors to develop, like marinating.

Preheat your grill to high (450°F [230°C]) for 3 to 5 minutes. You want the grill to be hot to sear the meat and not stick. Reduce the heat to medium and apply oil spray to the grate. Grill the kabobs on one side until well marked, about 2 minutes, flip and cook for another 2 minutes for medium (135°F [57°C] internal temperature) or your desired doneness. Remove from the skewers and place 3 keftas on each of 6 plates.

Spoon the sauce into a small serving bowl. Serve the keftas with the sauce or your favorite Mediterranean dip, such as hummus.

Ready-When-You-Are Braised Beef Short Ribs

Every great cook needs a braised short rib recipe in their repertoire. The dish is famous and the technique of braising is essential. The key to success is patience. Take your time browning the short ribs. Then, when deglazing the pan, allow all the wine to evaporate until almost a syrup. Finally, cook the ribs in the oven. It will all be worth it in the end. We love this dish with Super Fluffy and Buttery Mashed Potatoes (page 147).

Serves 4

Bouquet Garni
2 sprigs fresh parsley
2 sprigs fresh sage
2 sprigs fresh rosemary
2 sprigs fresh thyme

2 lb (910 g) beef short ribs, cut 2" (5 cm) thick
1 tbsp (18 g) kosher salt
2 tsp (6 g) black pepper
½ cup (60 g) all-purpose flour
Vegetable oil, such as canola, for frying
2 carrots, diced
1 large onion, diced
2 celery stalks, diced
2 cloves garlic, smashed
2 bay leaves, fresh preferred
2 cups (470 ml) red wine
2 cups (470 ml) beef stock

To make the bouquet garni, tie all the herbs together with kitchen twine. Set aside.

Season the beef thoroughly with the salt and pepper. Spread the flour in a shallow bowl, then dredge the beef well in the flour, shaking off the excess.

In a Dutch oven or other heavy-bottomed pot, heat 2 tablespoons (30 ml) of oil over medium-high to about 450°F (230°C). When white smoke first appears, place the short ribs in the Dutch oven and brown on all sides (in batches if necessary), turning occasionally. Remove after about 6 to 10 minutes, when the short ribs are a deep golden brown in color.

Add the carrots, onion, celery, garlic and bay leaves to the pot. Stir occasionally to brown, 4 to 6 minutes, but do not burn the aromatics.

Deglaze the pot with the red wine. Scrape lightly with a wooden spoon so that the brown bits on the bottom of the pan are released and become part of the sauce. Add the beef stock and bouquet garni and return the short ribs to the pot. Bring to a boil, then reduce to a simmer.

Simmer for about 2 hours, then check for tenderness. Remove the bouquet garni and bay leaves from the pot before serving the ribs with the sauce.

Chef Tip: Braised short ribs taste better with time. Store the cooked short ribs in the braising liquid. As they cool, they absorb the liquid and get even juicer. When ready to serve, warm them slowly in the braising liquid.

Shortcut Korean BBQ Short Ribs Worth Showing Off

The classic Korean cut of a three-bone piece of short rib is called a "flanken" cut. If you are not at an Asian market, tell any butcher you want ½-inch (1.3-cm) thick flanken-cut short ribs. Korean BBQ pros like myself love a slightly chewy texture, but it's not for everyone. If that makes you cringe a little, use any steak cut of beef, such as flank, New York strip or even rib eye. The secret to tender grilled short ribs is using apple or pear and Coca-Cola®. The fruit and the soda help break down the beef. This recipe was in my first cookbook, *101 Asian Dishes You Need to Cook Before You Die*, and it's such a perfect, classic Korean dish that it deserves a spot here. It's great by itself or served with rice or rice/grain blends. Add some gochujang or chile sauce and the recipe gets spicy.

Serves 4

Marinade

¼ cup (60 ml) soy sauce (I prefer regular, but low-sodium is fine)

¼ cup (60 ml) Coca-Cola Classic®

3 tbsp (36 g) packed brown sugar

1 tbsp (15 ml) toasted sesame oil

2 cloves garlic, finely minced

½ apple or pear, grated on a box grater

2 lb (910 g) flanken-cut short ribs

2 scallions, very finely sliced on an angle

1 tbsp (8 g) toasted sesame seeds

To make the marinade, combine the soy sauce, Coke, brown sugar, oil, garlic and grated apple in a large bowl. Using a whisk or fork, stir until the sugar is dissolved and the garlic is evenly distributed.

Add the short ribs to the bowl and massage the marinade into the beef. Cover the bowl with plastic, place in the fridge and allow the short ribs to marinate for 1 to 4 hours or up to 24 hours.

Heat a grill to its highest setting for at least 5 minutes. If using a charcoal or gas grill, wipe down the grill grates with a lightly oiled towel right before cooking to clean off any char and debris. This will give you a great grill mark and help keep the beef from sticking.

Remove the bowl of ribs from the refrigerator and pat any marinade off the ribs. Grill for about 4 minutes on each side, or until your desired doneness. Remove from the grill and garnish with the scallion and sesame seeds.

Chef Tip: As with papaya, Asian pears contain an enzyme that helps tenderize meat. Consider using it in your next meat marinade or braise. You can grind some Asian pears in a food processor and add it to your braised short ribs or stews.

Flank Steak with Chimichurri Sauce

The hallmarks to perfect grilled steaks are a great charred crust with some grill marks, seasoning generously and nailing the temperature (doneness). Always consider the thickness of the steak when cooking, knowing the thicker the steak, the longer the cook time (see the Chef Tips below). Chimichurri is a great sauce to know because it belongs to a group of uncooked condiments that touch so many cultures and dishes. If you can make chimichurri, you can make salsa verde and pesto. A rule of thumb is chimichurri is herbal, salsa verde is acidic and pesto is nutty. Choose the right sauce to pair perfectly with your protein or vegetable. Flank steak is a heavily used muscle but will grill amazingly. It's pleasantly chewy with great flavor.

Serves 4

Chimichurri Sauce
1 cup (60 g) packed fresh parsley
3 tbsp (8 g) chopped cilantro
1 tsp dried oregano
3 cloves garlic, finely minced
½ cup (120 ml) olive oil
¼ cup (60 ml) red wine vinegar
¼ tsp crushed red pepper flakes
1 tsp Maldon salt

Steak
2 lb (910 g) flank steak
Salt and freshly ground pepper, to taste
2 tbsp (30 ml) olive oil
1 tbsp (15 ml) soy sauce
1 large red onion, sliced into ½" (1.3-cm) rings

To make the chimichurri sauce, add all the sauce ingredients to a small food processor. Pulse 4 to 6 times, until the herbs are roughly chopped and chunky. Transfer to a serving bowl.

To make the steak, pat the flank steak dry with a paper towel. Season generously with salt and a pinch of pepper. Place in a medium-size bowl and drizzle with the olive oil and soy sauce. Add the onion to the bowl and give it all a massage until combined.

Heat a grill to high for at least 5 minutes. If using a charcoal or gas grill, wipe the grill grates with a lightly oiled paper towel right before cooking to clean off any char and debris. This will give you a great grill mark and help keep the beef from sticking.

Grill the steak for about 3 minutes, or until well browned on one side. Turn the steak over and add the onion to the grill. Cook for another 2 minutes, or until the internal temperature reaches 125°F (52°C) for medium-rare, or to your desired doneness (see the Chef Tips). You just want the onions slightly charred but still crunchy. Transfer the steak and onions to a cutting board and allow to rest, tented with foil, for 5 minutes. Slice the steak against the grain into 1-inch (2.5-cm) planks. Serve the steak over the onions and drizzle with the chimichurri sauce.

Chef Tips: Flank is thin, so use very high heat to get a good char in the short time it will take the steak to cook. Also, flank is so thin that a thermometer might not give you a good reading, so the press test will help. Take your index and poke a flank steak to measure its texture. If it feels and bounces back like poking your cheek, that's rare. Your firm chin is medium-rare. The firm, unyielding tip of your nose is well-done. With thicker steaks, use a thermometer and refer back to page 17 to test for doneness.

Flank steak also goes by the name carne asada. You can also substitute skirt steak for this recipe. This cut is best cooked rare to medium-rare. Any further cooking will be really tough to eat.

Low and Slow Prime Rib Roast with Horseradish Cream Sauce

The reverse-sear method is our method of choice for prime rib. Cooking the prime rib at a low temperature guarantees it will cook at a uniform rate, giving you a beautiful, evenly pink medium-rare all the way through, rather than the tree-ring coloring that happens when cooking at higher temperatures. This also keeps the prime rib super moist. Once you get the prime rib to the desired temperature, it can just rest for hours until you're ready to serve. When ready, fire up the oven, brown the meat and eat!

Serves 4–6

1 (5-lb [2.3-kg]) prime rib roast
3–4 tbsp (56–72 g) seasoned salt
2 tbsp (16 g) ground black pepper
2 tsp (2 g) dried thyme

Horseradish Cream Sauce
1 cup (240 g) sour cream
¼ cup (60 g) grated fresh horseradish
1 tbsp (11 g) Dijon mustard
1 tsp white wine vinegar
½ tsp kosher salt
¼ tsp freshly ground black pepper

Line a half sheet pan with parchment paper, place a wire rack on top and place the prime rib on the rack. Pat the prime rib dry with paper towels. Season the roast generously with salt, pepper and thyme. Refrigerate the roast, uncovered, for 1 to 2 days before you cook it. This will give it a crispy, dark brown crust.

To make the horseradish cream sauce, place all the ingredients in a medium-size mixing bowl and whisk until the mixture is smooth and creamy. Place in the refrigerator for at least 4 hours or overnight to allow the flavors to meld. The sauce can be stored in the refrigerator in an airtight container for 2 to 3 weeks.

Preheat the oven to 250°F (120°C). When ready to cook the prime rib, remove it from the fridge—no need to bring the roast to room temperature. Cook the roast for 2½ to 3 hours, until it reaches your desired doneness and temperature. For rare, cook to 125 to 130°F (52 to 54°C). Medium-rare is 130 to 135°F (54 to 57°C). Medium-well is 135 to 140°F (57 to 60°C). If you cook any further, why did you bother buying prime rib?

Pull the rib roast out of the oven and tent it with foil. The prime rib can rest for 30 minutes and up to 2 hours. When your guests are ready to eat, raise the temperature of the oven to 500°F (260°C) and roast the meat until you get a golden brown crust, 20 to 30 minutes. Another benefit of the reverse sear is you won't need to rest the meat again. Carve away and save me an end cut, please!

> **Chef Tips:** For great golden brown crust, season the prime rib and store in the fridge, uncovered, for up to 2 days. This will reduce the moisture in the prime rib and concentrate the flavors and give you a gorgeous bark.
>
> If you're not sure how much prime rib to prepare, plan on 1 pound (454 g) per person; this will allow for some leftovers and big eaters.

CHICKEN AND POULTRY

Classic Recipes and Techniques for Cooking Everyone's Favorite Birds

People say all sorts of things taste like chicken. Rabbit tastes like chicken and snake tastes like chicken. If that's the case, they are cooking chicken all wrong! The truth is, only chicken should taste like chicken—and it's delicious! No other meat is consumed more in the United States, and it's second in the world. In fact, there are almost 19 billion chickens farmed for food all over the world.

From a chef's perspective, we break poultry into two categories. Dark meat includes the legs, thighs and wings. These muscles do a lot of work, so they have more red blood cells and are tougher. Unlike with other animals, you don't have to cook the dark meat any longer. It's still relatively tender to eat without long braising or boiling. The muscle tissues are tiny and less tough compared to huge animals like cows or pigs. Then there's the white meat, which includes the breast. This muscle is lower in fat and very mild in flavor. You don't need to change cooking methods based on the part of the chicken.

Cooking turkey is like cooking two totally different animals. Like chicken, there's a difference in dark meat to white meat, but the differences are night and day. Turkey breast is super lean and drier tasting, while the dark meat is more gamey and tougher than chicken. Roasting and in soup are the best ways to enjoy this bird.

Duck is gamier and has the most fat of the three birds we are focusing on in this chapter. Unlike chickens, which mostly use their legs to get around and don't really fly, ducks fly and swim to get around. The more the muscles work, the more flavor you're going to get. The fat comes from living in colder weather and seeps through to their feathers to create waterproofing. Duck is richer and tougher, especially the dark meat. Duck is great for both moist and dry heat cooking.

In this chapter, we'll show you all the techniques to make chicken, turkey and duck taste like they're supposed to—delicious! Ali and I are like Jack Sprat and his wife: she only eats breasts and I only eat everything but breasts. We each specialize in our favorite parts of the bird. Poultry is pretty amazing because it's very versatile. It yields delicious flavor to both moist and dry heat. You can and should also use the entire bird (except for the feathers, of course). But flesh, bones, skin, gizzards, hearts and everything in between are usable and delicious. From boiling, which makes great soup, to roasting, frying and braising, poultry is a chef's culinary MacGyver.

Old-School Shake and Fry Buttermilk Fried Chicken

What's more comforting than fried chicken? Nailing the combination of crispy skin and moist and flavorful texture is the challenge. So, you need to have a two-pronged plan. Brining is simply soaking the chicken in a salty liquid. The best liquid for brine, in my and many others' opinion, is buttermilk. It's slightly acidic, which helps tenderize the bird and adds a pleasant tang to the meat. The seasoned salt dissolves into the brine and is carried into the protein via equilibrium. When submerged, the chicken is actually trading liquid with the brine. It plumps up and traps the salt, which gives it flavor and tenderness. There's a lot of science to fried chicken.

The brine will also help hold onto the flour. To get a crispy, flavorful, crunchy bite, be sure to season your flour. The seasoned flour will grip onto the buttermilk, which grips onto the chicken once fried and makes an amazing crust!

Serves 10

4 cups (960 ml) buttermilk

3 tbsp (45 g) Lawry's Seasoned Salt, divided

Black pepper, to taste

1 (3–3½-lb [1.4–1.6-kg]) fryer chicken, cut into 10 pieces

Oil, for frying

2 cups (240 g) all-purpose flour

Stir together the buttermilk, 2 tablespoons (30 g) of the seasoned salt and a heavy pinch of pepper in a large bowl until combined. Place the chicken pieces into the bowl, turn to coat well and cover tightly with plastic wrap. Refrigerate overnight or up to 2 days. The acidity from the buttermilk will tenderize the chicken while the salt penetrates the protein and gives great flavor.

When ready to fry, fill a large, heavy-bottomed 5- to 6-quart (4.5- to 5.4-L) Dutch oven halfway with oil and heat over medium-high heat to 365°F (185°C). Leave a frying thermometer in the pot to monitor the heat.

Shake together the flour, remaining 1 tablespoon (15 g) of seasoned salt and 1 teaspoon pepper in a 1- to 2-gallon (3.6- to 7.2-L) zip-top bag until well combined.

Place a cooling rack on top of a half sheet pan. Remove about half the chicken from the marinade and place in the plastic bag filled with the flour mixture. Close the top and shake to coat for about 10 seconds. Remove the chicken from the bag, knock off the excess flour and place on a plate. Do the same for the other half of the chicken and set aside.

Fry 3 to 4 pieces at a time for 6 to 10 minutes, or until golden brown and the internal temperature reaches 160°F (71°C). Drain on the cooling rack and repeat until all the chicken is cooked. If you've reached golden brown deliciousness but the chicken isn't hitting 160°F (71°C), you can always finish in a 350°F (180°C) oven. You can also hold the cooked chicken in the oven if you're not eating for a while.

Chef Tip: You can buy cut chicken if you're not excited about cutting a whole chicken. If you like dark meat, use the legs, thighs and wings. If you are using only breast, be sure to cut large breasts into two or three pieces before frying.

Sweet, Spicy and Crispy Chicken Wings

The secret to perfect chicken wings is a super crunchy batter that stays that way! Oil temperature is key; 365°F (185°C) is a good starting temperature because once you add the cold wings, the oil temperature will come down to about 350°F (180°C), which is perfect. You want to make sure to get the internal wing temperature to 165°F (74°C) while not burning the batter. A frying and instant-read thermometer is mandatory for all frying of meat: one for the oil and the other to check the internal temperature. I love tempura flour because it contains either corn or tapioca starch as well as wheat flour (often all-purpose flour). Starches don't contain protein, which makes most flours heavy. Think about the combo of flours like caramel corn! All-purpose flour is the popcorn that gives structure and the starches are the candy shell. Together they create a crunch that holds for a long time!

Serves 4–6

Sauce
3 cups (705 ml) Thai sweet chile sauce

¾ cup (180 ml) Sriracha, or more to taste

Chicken Wings
12 whole chicken wings, cut in half at the joint, tips discarded

2 cups (240 g) tempura flour

2½ qt (2.4 L) vegetable oil, for frying

2 cups (260 g) cornstarch

To make the sauce, stir together the sweet chile sauce and Sriracha in a large bowl. Set aside. You will be frying the wings and rolling them in this sauce while hot.

To make the chicken wings, rinse the chicken wings under cold water, drain briefly and place in a shallow baking dish still wet. Sprinkle the wings evenly with the tempura flour and massage until a thin batter forms.

Heat a large 6-quart (5.4-L) Dutch oven or large pot over high heat and add the oil. Using a frying thermometer, bring the temperature of the oil to 365°F (185°C).

Pour the cornstarch into a separate large bowl. Dredge the chicken wings in the cornstarch, dust off the excess and fry the wings in three batches. Cook each batch for 8 to 10 minutes, turning occasionally, until cooked through and golden brown. The internal temperature should be 165°F (74°C).

Drain the wings on paper towels briefly and roll them in the prepared sauce. Serve hot.

> **Chef Tip:** Never coat anything fried and crispy with a water-based sauce like Buffalo, honey mustard or barbecue sauce because it will soak in and make the food soggy immediately. If you coat fried things in a fat- or sugar-based sauce, like teriyaki or honey, or in an oil-based sauce, you will have long-lasting crispiness.

Tender Turkey Meatballs

Every culture on earth has its version of a meatball. When you grind meat, season it and bind it, chefs call it forcemeat. Other examples of forcemeat are meatloaf, sausages and pâté. When you take a forcemeat and stuff it into something like a dumpling or vegetable, such as stuffed cabbage or stuffed peppers, that forcemeat is now called a farce. To us, the secret to a great meatball is the actual grind of the forcemeat. What a lot of home cooks don't know is that you can actually request the size of the grind from your butcher for different dishes or applications. In a commercial grinder, the meat is chopped up and then pushed through holes, or a "die." I prefer a larger die grind for meatballs. It feels meatier and it's more delicious. You can substitute any protein you like for this recipe and have great results.

Makes 24 meatballs, serves 8

3 slices wheat sandwich bread, crusts removed (stale is fine)

⅓ cup (80 ml) milk

1 lb (454 g) ground turkey

1 lb (454 g) ground beef

½ cup (80 g) finely chopped onion

1¼ cups (125 g) finely grated Parmesan, preferably Parmigiano-Reggiano, divided

¼ cup (15 g) chopped fresh parsley

1 tsp dried oregano leaves, crumbled by hand

2 cloves garlic, finely chopped

1 tbsp (18 g) kosher salt

1 tsp black pepper

Olive oil, for frying

1 recipe Easy Homemade Tomato Sauce (page 37), for serving

1 recipe Creamy Polenta (page 36), for serving

Shaved Parmesan cheese, for serving

Preheat the oven to 350°F (180°C).

Tear the bread into small pieces and place in a large bowl. Pour the milk over the bread and let stand until the liquid is almost absorbed, 5 to 10 minutes.

To the same bowl, add the turkey, beef, onion, ¼ cup (25 g) of the Parmesan, parsley, oregano, garlic, salt and pepper. Work the mixture together with your fingers until just combined. (Tip: Overworking the meat will make the meatballs tough.) Form the meat into 24 golf ball–size rounds, about 1.75 ounces (50 g) each. (Note: You can make the meatballs a day ahead, cover and refrigerate before frying.)

Add ¼ inch (6 mm) of oil to a large skillet and bring the heat up to 375°F (190°C). Fry the meatballs in batches. Turn occasionally, until all sides are golden brown, 8 to 10 minutes per batch. Transfer the fried meatballs to a 9 x 13–inch (23 x 33–cm) baking dish and sprinkle with the remaining 1 cup (100 g) of Parmesan. Bake for about 15 minutes, or until the internal temperature reaches 165°F (74°C).

Heat the tomato sauce. On each of 8 plates, spoon about 1 cup (240 g) of polenta in the middle of the plate. Place 3 meatballs on top of the polenta. Top with about ½ cup (120 ml) of tomato sauce. Finish with shaved Parmesan cheese.

Chef Tip: The difference between Parmigiano-Reggiano and Parmesan cheese is that Parmigiano-Reggiano is the real deal. It is made in Italy according to a specific recipe.

Creamy Polenta

Polenta is a fancy term for corn porridge made from stone-ground dried corn. Americans call it grits and Italians call it polenta. Understanding the cooking and hydration of dried grains is a skill you will use many times in your cooking life. Learning to cook polenta is important! If you can cook polenta, you can make many other grains, like grits, quinoa, farro and couscous. The more liquid you add, the softer and creamier the grains become. Add less liquid and they can harden into solid planks that eat like thick starchy cakes, which are perfect for serving with savory meat dishes. This recipe is for making soft, creamy polenta. Water makes the grains soft and Parmesan gives the final dish a great creamy cheesiness!

Serves 8

4 cups (960 ml) water

1 tsp salt, plus more to taste

1 cup (140 g) polenta or yellow cornmeal

¼ cup (56 g) unsalted butter

½ cup (50 g) grated Parmesan cheese

Pepper, to taste

In a medium-size saucepan, bring the water to a boil. Add the salt and rain in the polenta while constantly whisking. Keep whisking until the polenta is smooth and starts to thicken. Reduce the heat to low and cook for about 30 minutes, until tender and creamy, stirring often. Stir in the butter and Parmesan cheese until thoroughly incorporated. Season to taste with salt and pepper.

Chef Tip: Cornmeal cooks faster than polenta and takes about half the time. You want to cook the grains for at least 20 to 30 minutes so they break down and feel creamy, similar to cooking risotto.

Easy Homemade Tomato Sauce

This is your go-to homemade tomato sauce recipe that is good for everything—pasta, pizza, meatballs and more. I always have a quart (1 L) on hand for quick meals. Anchovies are instant umami. They add a rich savoriness to any dish and cooking them in the pan before adding the tomatoes makes them melt right in and gives the sauce a delicious boost, so don't be scared to try it. Cooking also helps remove the tin-can flavor from the tomatoes. If you want a very smooth sauce, run it through a blender.

Makes 4 cups (960 ml)

¼ cup (60 ml) extra virgin olive oil

2 tsp (7 g) minced garlic

4 anchovy fillets, rough chopped (optional)

2 (28-oz [784-g]) cans diced tomatoes, drained

2 tsp (2 g) dried oregano

1 tsp kosher salt

¼ tsp freshly ground black pepper

2 tsp (8 g) sugar (optional, see Chef Tip)

Heat the olive oil in a deep skillet over medium-high heat. When the temperature gets to about 375°F (190°C), stir in the garlic and the anchovies and sizzle for about 30 seconds.

Pour in the tomatoes, bring to a simmer and cook for about 10 minutes, until the sauce reduces and thickens slightly. Lower the heat if the sauce starts to boil. Stir in the oregano, salt, pepper and sugar, if using, and cook for an additional minute. Remove the sauce from the heat and use immediately or store in airtight containers or even zip-top bags in the refrigerator or freezer until ready to use.

Chef Tip: Believe it or not, most chefs like high-quality canned tomatoes over fresh. Canned tomatoes from Italy are picked at the peak of ripeness and are far better than tasteless fresh tomatoes out of season. Buy crushed or chopped Italian canned tomatoes for this dish. If you have to use a domestic canned tomato or tomatoes out of season, add a pinch of sugar to the sauce. Ripe tomatoes have a lot more sweetness and don't need the sugar.

Family Dinner Roast Chicken with Shallots and Tarragon

Every cook needs to know how to roast a perfect chicken. There are three critical steps: 1. Season the bird inside and out with a dry or wet brine. I like dry because it means fewer steps and most birds are already pumped with saline and will therefore be moist. 2. Dry the bird overnight in the fridge to get perfect crispy and delicious skin. 3. Learn a simple pan sauce made from pan drippings, herbs and butter. Once you master the chicken, these same steps can be applied to any roast beast.

Serves 4–6

1 (3½–4-lb [1.6–1.8-g]) whole chicken

2 tsp (12 g) kosher salt, plus more to taste

½ tsp freshly ground black pepper, plus more to taste

3 medium shallots, quartered

6 medium cloves garlic, crushed

2–3 tarragon sprigs plus 1 tbsp (4 g) chopped tarragon, divided

4 tbsp (56 g) unsalted butter, 2 tbsp (28 g) softened, remaining 2 tbsp (28 g) chilled and cut into 2 pieces, divided

Pan spray

Chef Tip: "Dry brining" simply means seasoning the bird and letting it marinate rather than submerging it completely in a saltwater solution. Air-drying in the fridge uncovered helps make the skin super golden brown and delicious.

The day before serving, generously season the inside of the bird with the salt and pepper, then place the shallot quarters, garlic and tarragon sprigs in the cavity of the chicken.

Take the 2 tablespoons (28 g) of softened butter with gloved hands and rub the bird generously inside and out, covering the bird with a thin coating. Season generously with salt and pepper. Gather the skin on both sides of the cavity and thread a bamboo skewer through flaps of skin to sew it the best you can. Don't worry about trying to make a surgical stitch. Place on a parchment-lined half sheet pan. Refrigerate overnight, uncovered, to allow the skin to air-dry.

One hour before roasting, take the chicken out of the refrigerator to allow it to come up to room temperature. Set the oven shelf to the lower-middle position and preheat the oven to 375°F (190°C). Spray a roasting rack with cooking spray and set in a half sheet pan or other roasting pan.

Roast the chicken for 40 to 50 minutes, or until the thickest part of the thigh registers 165 to 170°F (74 to 77°C) on an instant-read thermometer. Carefully remove the pan from the oven; tip the bird to let the juices from the cavity run into the roasting pan. Transfer the chicken to a cutting board and let rest, uncovered, while making the sauce. Let the liquid rest so that the fat floats to the top, and pour off as much of the fat as possible.

Place a small saucepan over medium heat. Pour the reserved chicken juices and bits into the saucepan and bring to a boil. Reduce the sauce until thick, rich and brown in color. Add the remaining 1 tablespoon (4 g) of chopped tarragon and whisk in the remaining 2 tablespoons (28 g) of butter until it melts and makes a sauce. Taste and adjust the seasoning.

Break down the chicken into your desired pieces or cuts. You can roast under the broiler until the skin is crispy, if desired; serve hot with the warm pan sauce.

Perfectly Pan-Seared Duck Breast with Blackberry Gastrique

Every chef wants to nail the perfect cook on a duck breast—rendered crispy skin, seared on both sides and perfectly medium-rare in the middle. There are a few key steps to doing this right. One key is to score the skin but not go through to the actual "meat" muscle of the duck. Next, you want to finish in an oven instead of on top of the stove. In addition, doneness needs to be measured with a thermometer for the first hundred times you do it. You'll eventually learn the feel of perfect medium-rare. Finally, let your duck breast rest for a few minutes before slicing. Resting will keep the juices in and keep the duck moist!

I love serving duck with a gastrique, which is just a fancy term for a sweet and sour sauce. Adding tart fruit, like blackberries in this recipe, gives another flavor dimension to a gastrique. A proper gastrique should be slightly sticky, thickened by reducing the sauce. This berry gastrique is amazing with rich meats like duck, beef and pork. You can substitute your favorite berry, such as blueberries or raspberries, and frozen berries work great, too.

Serves 4

Blackberry Gastrique
½ cup (100 g) sugar
2 tbsp (30 ml) water
½ cup (120 ml) red wine vinegar
⅔ cup (92 g) blackberries
1 tsp fresh lemon juice
½ tsp kosher salt

2 (5–6-oz [140–168-g]) duck breasts
Maldon salt and ground black pepper, to taste

Chef Tips: Reserved duck fat is like liquid gold. It's awesome for frying potatoes, cooking eggs and used anywhere you would use butter.

I like to air-dry the duck breasts the day before cooking by keeping them in the fridge uncovered.

Maldon salt is our favorite seasoning salt for this dish.

To make the gastrique, combine the sugar and water in a small, heavy-bottomed saucepan. Cook over medium-high heat until the sugar is dissolved. Continue to cook without stirring until the liquid reaches a light blond caramel color, 5 to 8 minutes, swirling gently to help the mixture cook evenly. Carefully add the red wine vinegar and berries all at once (the mixture will boil very rapidly). Continue to cook until the sugar dissolves again, about 3 minutes.

Cook until reduced and slightly syrupy, like maple syrup, 2 to 3 minutes. If it becomes too thick, stir in 1 teaspoon of water at a time until you reach the perfect viscosity. Remove from the heat and add the lemon juice and kosher salt. You can use immediately or cover tightly until ready to use.

Preheat the oven to 400°F (200°C). Season the duck on all sides with salt and pepper.

Pat each duck breast dry with paper towels. Score the fat on top of the duck in a crosshatch pattern, being careful to score only the fat and not cutting the flesh beneath it.

Set an ovenproof, nonstick skillet over medium-high heat. Immediately place the duck, skin-side down, in the cold pan. After a few minutes, the fat from the skin will start to render out. Periodically drain the excess fat into a small, heatproof bowl to save it (see Chef Tips). After 10 to 12 minutes, the skin should be golden brown and crispy, while the meat will still be uncooked.

After the skin reaches a golden brown, flip the duck breasts over skin-side up. Place the skillet in the oven and cook for 7 to 10 minutes, or until the internal temperature reaches 132°F (56°C). Let the duck breasts rest on a cutting board for 10 minutes before slicing.

Slice the duck on an angle into tiles. Serve with the gastrique and a pinch each of Maldon salt and pepper.

Holiday Herb-Brined Roasted Whole Turkey with Gravy

Every good cook needs to know how to roast a turkey for the holidays. Practice will make perfect. Don't be daunted by the size of the bird. Give yourself ample days to defrost it in the fridge if buying frozen. I am a believer in brining to keep the turkey moist and seasoned. I'll also show you how to make a gravy and cranberry sauce to go with it.

Serves 14–16

Brine
2 cups (470 ml) hot water
2 cups (576 g) kosher salt
1 cup (225 g) packed brown sugar
3 sprigs fresh sage
Zest of 1 orange, removed in large pieces
2 gal (7.2 L) ice-cold water

Turkey
1 (14–16-lb [6.4–7.3-kg]) fresh turkey
½ cup (112 g) unsalted butter, softened
Zest of 1 orange
Zest of 1 lemon
8 large sage leaves, minced
1 tsp salt
1 orange, quartered
1 lemon, quartered
1 onion, quartered
4 cloves garlic, peeled and left whole
4–5 sprigs fresh parsley
1½ cups (355 ml) turkey stock, plus more as needed
2 tbsp (16 g) all-purpose flour
1 tbsp (15 ml) dry sherry
Salt and freshly ground pepper, to taste

To make the brine, in a large pot, combine the hot water, salt and brown sugar and stir until the salt and sugar are dissolved. Add the fresh sage, orange zest and cold water and stir to combine.

To make the turkey, line an extra-large stockpot with a large, heavy plastic bag (about 30-gallon [108-L] capacity). Rinse the turkey, place it in the plastic bag and pour the brine over the turkey. Gather the plastic bag tightly around the turkey so that the bird is covered with brine, then seal the plastic bag. Refrigerate the pot with the turkey in the brine for at least 12 hours and up to 18 hours.

Preheat the oven to 325°F (170°C).

Remove the turkey from the brine and rinse VERY well inside and out. Pat dry. In a small food processor, combine the butter, citrus zests, sage and salt and process until very well combined.

Use your hand to separate the skin from the flesh of the turkey around the breasts and liberally rub the butter mixture in this area. Fill the cavity with the citrus quarters, onion, garlic and parsley, then pin the cavity back together with a skewer and tie the legs together with twine. Fold the smallest part of the wings back to sit under the turkey to avoid burning. Place the turkey on a roasting rack in a heavy-bottomed roasting pan, breast-side up. Rub the top of the breast skin with a bit of the butter mixture and cover this area only VERY TIGHTLY with foil. Add the stock to the bottom of the pan.

Transfer to the oven and roast the turkey for 3¼ to 4 hours, or until a thermometer inserted into the thigh reads 165°F (74°C). For the last hour, remove the foil and baste with the pan drippings often. During roasting, if the pan starts to dry up, add more turkey stock. Remove the turkey from the oven and from the pan and place it on a carving board. Brush with the pan drippings again and cover with foil. (Note: It's important the turkey rest for at least 20 minutes before carving. Resting will allow the juices to stay in the bird, making it juicy and moist.)

To Serve

Cranberry Sauce (page 44)

Wild Rice with Almonds and Dried Cranberries (page 86)

Super Fluffy and Buttery Mashed Potatoes (page 147)

In the meantime, to make the gravy, remove the pan drippings and pour into a larger separator. Strain the liquid into a measuring cup and add enough turkey stock to make about 6 cups (1.4 L). Measure ¼ cup (60 ml) of the fat from the top of the liquid. Place the roasting pan on top of two burners on the stove over medium heat. Add the fat to the pan and whisk in the flour. Cook until the flour has just begun to brown, about 3 minutes. Whisk in the measured stock and drippings and the sherry. Cook over low heat, whisking constantly, until the gravy begins to simmer and thicken, about 1 to 2 minutes. Taste; there should be no taste of flour. Season with salt and pepper and remove from the heat. Serve immediately with cranberry sauce, wild rice and mashed potatoes.

Chef Tip: If you're not sure how much turkey to buy per person, buy 1 pound (454 g) per person to be safe. That will make for a great meal plus enough leftovers for a second delicious meal.

Cranberry Sauce

This is another essential recipe for the holidays and it's so much better made from scratch. It requires a handful of ingredients and can be cooked in 30 minutes. You can make this sauce up to a week before you need it. It gets better with time. Don't you dare buy the canned gelatinous stuff!

Makes 3 cups (675 g)

2 cups (400 g) sugar

1½ cups (355 ml) orange juice

6 cloves

6 allspice berries

4 (3-inch [7.5-cm]) cinnamon sticks

2 (12-oz [340-g]) bags fresh cranberries

Grated zest of 2 oranges

Combine the sugar, orange juice, cloves, allspice and cinnamon sticks in a 4-quart (3.6-L) saucepan over medium heat. Cook, stirring, until the syrup is clear, about 3 minutes.

Add the fresh cranberries, turn up the heat and bring to a boil for about 5 minutes, until the cranberries begin to pop. Remove from the heat, add the grated orange zest and let cool. Don't panic if the sauce doesn't look even immediately. It will take a few days to cure, getting to that dark syrupy, ruby red color.

Refrigerate for 1 to 3 days before serving. Remove the cloves, allspice and cinnamon sticks before serving.

Chef Tip: This cranberry sauce is not just for turkey and ham. We love serving this over pumpkin pie and ice cream as well, so be sure to put this sauce out with the desserts.

Tender and Crispy Duck Confit

Confit is a culinary term that translates to "preserve." Food is preserved by cooking at a low temperature in fat, juice or oil. This removes all the air, brings the meat to a safe temperature and then seals it in liquid. The most popular type of confit is duck, which is cooked in fat. But you can confit just about anything. Other popular confits are fruit preserves, potted meats, fish and leeks. Duck confit has many uses. Serve these legs as a main protein with a side vegetable. Crumble it onto salads to make a meal. Flake it as a filling for ravioli, dumplings or tacos. It's one of my favorite things to eat!

Serves 4

1½ tbsp (27 g) kosher salt

½ tsp ground bay leaves

½ tsp ground thyme

½ tsp ground allspice

½ tsp crushed juniper berries

1 tbsp (8 g) cracked black pepper

4 duck leg and thigh quarters, about 2 lb (910 g)

8 cloves garlic, peeled

2 cups (470 ml) rendered duck fat or olive oil

Combine the salt, bay, thyme, allspice, juniper berries and pepper in a small bowl. Spread over the duck legs and allow to cure, uncovered, in the refrigerator for 2 days.

When ready to cook, preheat the oven to 250°F (120°C).

Remove the duck legs from the refrigerator, brush off the excess spices and place the duck in an ovenproof, covered casserole or Dutch oven that holds them snugly. Add the garlic. Warm the duck fat in a saucepan and pour enough into the casserole to cover the duck legs. Cover with the lid.

Place in the oven and bake for about 3 hours, until the duck meat has retracted up the drumstick bone and the meat is very tender. Remove from the oven and allow to cool with the lid off.

Cover and refrigerate overnight or for up to 10 days in the casserole.

To serve, remove the duck legs from the fat and remove and reserve the excess fat. Heat 2 teaspoons (10 ml) of the duck fat in a sauté pan over high heat. At the first sign of white smoke, which will be about 450°F (230°C), place the duck legs in the pan skin-side down. Cook until the skin is golden brown and crispy, then turn once and cook on the other side for about 1 minute, until warmed through. Serve skin-side up.

Chef Tips: Always save duck fat! Strain the fat and use it for the next time you make confit. Or use it to cook potatoes. If you don't have any in reserve, duck fat can be found in gourmet stores or even online. But don't be discouraged if you can't source duck fat. Olive oil will work just fine.

If there's any jellied stock at the bottom, it's concentrated (and seasoned) duck stock. Use it anywhere you would use chicken stock (although adjust the total salt accordingly).

This dish is perfect served with a hearty salad, lentils or roasted potatoes.

Better-Than-Takeout Orange Chicken

For those of you who bought my first book, you may recognize this one. It was one of the most popular dishes in that book and it's a recipe people constantly ask for. There are two secrets to crispy chicken stir-fry, and the first is how you dredge and fry it. You want a light, crispy batter that contains cornstarch or potato starch and all-purpose flour. Both are already contained in store-bought tempura flour. If you can't find it, just combine 1 cup (120 g) of all-purpose flour, 1 cup (120 g) of cornstarch and 1 tablespoon (8 g) of baking soda. The next secret is the sauce has to have a good amount of sugar to make a syrup. A syrup won't make crispy batter soggy. As with most recipes, feel free to substitute another meat or protein for the chicken.

Serves 4

Perfect Jasmine Rice (page 84),
for serving

Orange-Flavored Sauce
½ cup (120 ml) oyster sauce
1 tbsp (15 ml) hoisin sauce
6 tbsp (90 ml) orange juice
½ cup (100 g) sugar
6 tbsp (90 ml) white vinegar
2 tbsp (30 ml) soy sauce
½ tbsp (4 g) ground paprika
½ tbsp (4 g) minced ginger
2 cloves garlic, minced
1 tbsp (7 g) cornstarch mixed with
1 tbsp (15 ml) water
1 drop red food coloring (optional)

Chicken
1 qt (1 L) plus 2 tbsp (30 ml) vegetable
oil, divided
2 lb (910 g) chicken thighs, cut into
2" (5-cm) dice
1 cup (235 ml) cold water
2½ cups (300 g) tempura flour, divided
½ onion, cut into large dice
4 scallions, sliced into 2" (5-cm)
lengths

I like serving this with white rice. The rice should be cooked and resting while you are making the orange chicken, so if you're serving with rice, start that first.

To make the sauce, add all the sauce ingredients to a 1-quart (1-L) saucepan over medium heat. Whisk gently as it comes to a simmer. Allow to simmer, whisking constantly, for about 5 minutes, or until the sauce thickens. Remove from the heat and set aside.

To make the chicken, heat 1 quart (1 L) of the oil in a 4-quart (3.6-L) Dutch oven to 165°F (74°C) using a frying thermometer. Rinse the chicken under cold water and pat dry with paper towels.

In a medium-size bowl, combine the water and 1½ cups (180 g) of the tempura flour into a thick batter; it should look like a thick pancake batter. Spread the remaining 1 cup (120 g) of tempura flour on a plate. Dredge the chicken cubes in the tempura flour, coat in a thin layer of the batter, knock off the excess batter and fry in two batches until golden brown and crispy, 6 to 8 minutes. Drain on paper towels or a rack.

Heat the remaining 2 tablespoons (30 ml) of oil in a wok or large skillet over high heat. When you see the first wisps of white smoke, stir in the fried chicken, onion and scallions and cook for about 30 seconds. Stir in the sauce and allow to coat and simmer for a minute or two. Cook, folding with a spatula, until all the ingredients are well coated, about 2 minutes.

Sunday Night Chicken Parmesan

Paillard isn't just a dish; it's also a technique. The technique is to cut and pound a piece of meat into a thin, even piece, then bread and fry it, similar to scaloppini or piccata. Pounding meat thin helps it tenderize and makes it all one thickness, which guarantees moist, even cooking. We always have the ingredients for chicken Parm in the house for a quick family meal. You can paillard the chicken flat and hold it frozen. When ready to eat, just thaw, bread and cook very quickly. Add tomato sauce and cheese, serve with pasta and you'll have dinner in no time!

Serves 4

1 tbsp (18 g) kosher salt
2 tsp (6 g) black pepper
1 tbsp (6 g) Italian seasoning mix
2 lb (910 g) boneless, skinless chicken thighs
½ cup (60 g) all-purpose flour
3 large eggs, beaten
2–3 cups (230–345 g) panko bread crumbs
Canola oil, for frying
5 cups (1.2 L) Easy Homemade Tomato Sauce (page 37), divided
1 cup (100 g) finely grated Parmesan, divided
8 oz (224 g) fresh mozzarella, torn into bite-size pieces

Preheat the oven to 375°F (190°C).

Combine the kosher salt, pepper and Italian seasoning in a small bowl and set aside.

Take a heavy-duty zip-top bag and cut open one side of it. Place one or two cutlets at a time as flat as possible in the bag. Using a meat pounder, small frying pan or rolling pin, pound the meat to an even ¼ inch (6 mm) thick. Season each piece generously with the seasoning mix.

Separately, place the flour, eggs and panko into three wide, shallow bowls. Dip each paillard in the flour, then the eggs and then coat with the panko, pressing it in for thorough coverage.

Pour the oil into a large skillet to a depth of ½ inch (1.3 cm). Place over medium-high heat. When the oil reaches 375°F (190°C) on a frying thermometer, fry the cutlets in batches, turning halfway through, until golden brown, 2 to 4 minutes for each side. Transfer to a paper towel–lined plate.

Spread 4 cups (960 ml) of the tomato sauce over the bottom of a 9 x 13–inch (23 x 33–cm) baking pan. Sprinkle one-third of the Parmesan over the sauce. Place half of the cutlets over the Parmesan and top with the mozzarella pieces. Dot some of the remaining 1 cup (235 ml) of sauce sparingly over the mozzarella, then top with the remaining Parmesan. The idea here is to keep the crispy coating texture on top rather than making it soggy with too much sauce.

Transfer the pan to the oven and bake until the cheese is golden, the casserole is bubbling and the internal temperature of the chicken is 165°F (74°C), about 15 minutes. Remove from the oven and let cool for a few minutes before serving.

Variation: Eggplant Parmesan
To make eggplant Parmesan, substitute ½-inch (1.3-cm) thick slices of Italian eggplant for the chicken. You can also buy gluten-free panko bread crumbs and use gluten-free all-purpose flour if needed.

PORK

Chef Secrets to Mastering the King of Meats

To many chefs, pork is the king of meats! It gives us some of our most important culinary gems, like bacon, sausage and ribs. This animal is celebrated from ear to tail. From ham to pig ears, there are no bits or bobs that can't be made into a delicacy.

When it comes to pork, different parts cook differently and vary in taste. As with most four-legged animals, the muscles that are used the least are the most tender and can be cooked quickly, but they can dry out, too. You also usually trade tender for less flavor. The leaner, more tender cuts are loin, tenderloin and baby back ribs. The tougher or fatty parts like belly, leg, hocks and trotters are more flavorful. The trade-off is you have to cook them longer with moist heat. Then there are those perfect parts that balance tender with tough and fat with lean, like the shoulder and spareribs.

In this chapter, you'll master most of the popular parts. I'm going to teach you how to cook bacon like a chef and how to make pork chops flavorful but still moist. You will also learn how to make amazing pork ribs without having to use a smoker or wait hours and hours.

Let's be clear. The U.S. Food and Drug Administration guidelines are very strict about cooking all pork to at least 165°F (74°C). It's their job to keep all diners safe, and we appreciate that. If you look at the statistics over the years, the chances of getting sick eating undercooked pork are about the same as eating runny egg yolks or steak tartare. And those chances are super low. We are proponents of the medium-well pork movement. If you cook all pork to 165°F (74°C), the meat will be gray, dry and pretty bland. So buy your pork from a reputable source and cook it to 145 to 150°F (63 to 66°C), unless you're cooking it for a very long time to make it fall-apart tender.

No-Grill-Needed Baby Back Ribs

I didn't say the "B" word: barbecue. You need a smoker to make authentic barbecue, but a lot of us are perfectly happy with pull-apart tender, delicious and sweet ribs. The first trick is a dry rub. A combination of ground dry spices will bring deep flavor to the meat. The next trick is to bake the ribs wrapped in foil to create moist heat and let the ribs braise in the foil. After that, you want to baste with a great sauce and cook over direct heat to sear and lock that sauce onto the meat to create smokiness.

Serves 4–6

Barbecue Rub

6 tbsp (108 g) kosher salt

3 tbsp (36 g) packed dark brown sugar

3 tbsp (21 g) paprika

1 tbsp (9 g) granulated garlic powder

2 tbsp (14 g) granulated onion powder

2 tsp (5 g) ground cumin

1 tbsp (8 g) ground black pepper

1 tsp cayenne pepper, or to taste

4–5 lb (1.8–2.3 kg) baby back ribs (2 full slabs)

Quick and Easy Barbecue Sauce

3 tbsp (30 g) Barbecue Rub (from above)

1 cup (235 ml) red wine vinegar

1 cup (160 g) chopped yellow onion

2 tbsp (20 g) minced garlic

½ cup (112 g) packed light brown sugar

½ cup (160 g) molasses

2 cups (480 g) ketchup

To make the rub, in a small mixing bowl, combine all the seasonings. Set aside 3 tablespoons (30 g) of the rub to use in the sauce.

Place the ribs on a large baking sheet. Using a butter knife, pry up the thin membrane on the bone side of the ribs, called the fell. Using a paper towel for grip, pull to remove and discard.

Divide the remaining rub between the racks and rub well on all sides. Let the ribs sit undisturbed for at least 20 minutes and up to 8 hours; place in the refrigerator if marinating for longer than 20 minutes. Remove the ribs from the refrigerator and allow to come to room temperature for 1 hour before cooking.

To make the sauce, combine all of the ingredients in a blender and blend until smooth. Transfer to a nonreactive saucepan and simmer for 20 minutes to allow the flavors to marry. Keep warm to use in this dish, or refrigerate in a nonreactive, airtight container for up to 2 weeks.

Preheat your oven to 300°F (150°C). Tear off two large sheets of heavy-duty foil, large enough to wrap each rib completely, always keeping the shiny side toward the food. Brush each rack of ribs with 2 cups (480 g) of the sauce, making sure to brush it on both sides. Wrap tightly in the foil and bake for 2 hours and 30 minutes, or until tender and the internal temperature reaches 190°F (88°C).

Remove from the oven and allow to rest, covered, for at least 20 minutes. You can serve them out of the oven or brush the ribs with more sauce and grill or broil them in the oven just to make them sticky and lip smacking.

Chef Tips: If you have a smoker of any kind, first smoke these ribs at 225 to 250°F (107 to 120°C) for about 4 hours. Then, bathe them in sauce and grill for about 10 minutes.

For a quick smoke flavor hack, substitute smoked salt for the kosher salt.

Use only heavy-duty 18-inch (45-cm) wide foil; it won't tear and is wide enough for all kitchen jobs.

Oven-Cooked Bacon Like a Chef

Ovens are the key to making perfect bacon. Think about the millions of slices of bacon made every day in America, from homes to room service to restaurants. It would be a mess and impossible to cook it all in skillets. There would be grease fires all over the place. The oven is perfect because you can cook baking sheets upon sheets at a time at an even temperature. Once the bacon is done, you can drain off the fat and store until you're ready to eat. Most chefs cook the bacon until their desired doneness (crispy or floppy), then hold it in the fridge or on the line until needed. The same technique works great in the home kitchen and saves so much time and mess. You can rewarm or crisp in either a pan or oven again. It's the best for even, straight, perfect pieces of bacon.

Serves 4–6

1 (12-oz [340-g]) package thick-cut bacon

Preheat the oven to 400°F (200°C).

Line a cookie sheet or half sheet pan with aluminum foil. Lay out the bacon strips in a single layer. For super crispy bacon, cook on a rack over the sheet pan. Place in the oven. After 15 minutes, start watching the bacon for your preferred level of brownness, as it browns and crisps more quickly in the last few minutes, depending on the thickness of the bacon and desired level of crispiness. The bacon will be soft and floppy at 15 minutes and firm at about 22 to 25 minutes.

Remove from the pan to a rack or plates lined with paper towels. Serve what you want now, and allow the extra to cool. Keep the bacon drippings for cooking eggs, potatoes and steaks. Once the bacon has cooled, store in the fridge and reheat when needed.

> **Chef Tip:** Cook bacon once every week or two in the oven. Cook more than you need because it's bacon!

New Mexico Green Chile Stew

Stewing pork is different than beef. It breaks down faster and has more fat in the meat. Commercial pork also has more moisture than beef. Searing and then stewing is important because the technique is used a lot in cooking. Dishes like adobo, ragu and other Latin stews all use this technique. Ali makes this green chile stew when Hatch chiles are in season, and it's spectacular! I truly can't get enough of it. It has deep flavor with that warming spice of sweet green chiles. I never understood why folks went crazy for in-season Hatch chiles until I ate this stew. You can substitute any meat for the pork in this recipe. If using chicken, use thighs and cut them into larger pieces.

Serves 6–8

2 lb (910 g) boneless pork shoulder, cut into 1½'' (3.8-cm) cubes

2 tbsp (30 ml) olive oil

1 small onion, chopped

2 cloves garlic, minced

¼ cup (30 g) all-purpose flour

3 cups (540 g) peeled and diced plum tomatoes

2 cups (270 g) New Mexico green chiles, roasted, peeled and chopped

1 jalapeño pepper, minced

1 tsp ground cumin

1 tsp New Mexico green chile powder, or more to taste

½ tsp sugar

2 cups (470 ml) beef broth

1 tsp salt

½ tsp pepper

2 cups (300 g) medium-diced waxy potatoes

Warm tortillas or crusty bread, for serving

Heat a large Dutch oven over high heat for about 1 minute. Pat the pork cubes dry with a paper towel. Coat the bottom of the Dutch oven with the olive oil and add the pork to the pot. Sear on all sides until golden brown, about 5 minutes.

Stir in the onion and garlic and cook until translucent, 1 to 2 minutes. Stir in the flour and cook for an additional minute, until all the pork is coated evenly. Stir in the tomatoes, roasted chiles, jalapeño, cumin, New Mexico chile powder and sugar and cook for about 2 minutes, until combined.

Pour in the broth and add the salt and pepper. Cover and simmer over low heat for about 1½ hours, stirring every 20 minutes and making sure to scrape the bottom.

Stir in the potatoes and cook for about 30 minutes, or until fork tender. The pork will be tender and the stew will be nice and thick. Taste and adjust the seasoning to your liking. Serve with warm tortillas or crusty bread.

> **Chef Tip:** Canned green chiles will work great off-season. Also, you can get green chile powder all year long and I think it's a great way to get that distinct flavor when the chiles aren't in season.

Red Roasted Chinese BBQ Pork Chops

Red, sticky, sweet and savory Chinese barbecue is a gift from southern China. You can apply this authentic technique to the familiar pork chop. The teaching points here are to marinate your chops to get flavor in, roast to get that charred taste and then add honey to the marinade to make an amazing glaze. You must cook any marinade that has touched raw meat to make it safe. Bring the sauce to a boil, add the honey to create a thick glaze and then use it to baste and sauce the final dish.

Serves 4

Marinade
2 tbsp (30 ml) sherry
1 tbsp (6 g) minced fresh ginger
⅓ cup (80 ml) oyster sauce
½ tsp Chinese five-spice powder
½ cup (120 ml) soy sauce
¼ cup (50 g) sugar
6 tbsp (90 ml) hoisin sauce
6 tbsp (90 g) ketchup
2–4 drops red food coloring (optional)

Pork
2 lb (910 g) pork chops, at least 1" (2.5 cm) wide
4 tbsp (80 g) honey

To make the marinade, in a large bowl, stir together all the sauce ingredients. Set aside. (Note: Red food coloring will make your chops look like gorgeous Chinese barbecue. The flavor will be great without it, but that is how restaurants do it.)

To make the pork, place the pork chops in a shallow baking dish. Pour the marinade over the pork. Let the pork marinate for 4 hours and up to overnight in the refrigerator.

Preheat the oven to 400°F (200°C).

Drain the pork marinade into a small saucepan. Bring to a boil over high heat, then stir in the honey and cook until completely combined. Set aside for basting and plating.

Place the chops on a parchment-lined sheet pan. Roast for 10 minutes, then baste with the honey marinade mixture. Roast for 10 more minutes, or until golden brown and the internal temperature reaches 145°F (63°C). Remove from the oven and let rest for at least 8 minutes. Drizzle some sauce over the chops before serving.

Coca-Cola® Carnitas

I learned Coke was the secret to making carnitas during my many trips to Mexico visiting my family's produce farms. The sugar and caramel penetrate during braising and give the meat flavor and that golden brown delicious (GBD) color. Rumor has it that it also helps tenderize the pork, and I believe it. Carnitas is a versatile meat that makes a great filling for tacos, nachos, tortas, burritos and sopes. We always have it shredded in the freezer to cook up with scrambled eggs with onions, tomatoes and chiles in the morning. We call it pork-chaca, the piggy version of the beef dish machaca.

Serves 4

4–5 sprigs fresh oregano

4–5 sprigs fresh parsley

4–5 sprigs fresh thyme

½ cup (120 ml) vegetable oil or lard

2 lb (910 g) pork shoulder, cut into 4" (10-cm) cubes

2 tbsp (36 g) kosher salt, plus more for seasoning

½ onion, chopped

2 cloves garlic, crushed

2 bay leaves

3 tbsp (45 ml) orange juice

2 (14½-oz [406-g]) cans chicken stock

1½ cups (355 ml) Coca-Cola

¼ cup (60 ml) heavy cream

Tie the oregano, parsley and thyme into a bouquet garni with about 12 inches (30.5 cm) of butcher twine.

Heat the vegetable oil in a large Dutch oven over high heat. Season the pork shoulder generously with salt, then arrange in the Dutch oven. Cook until browned on all sides, about 10 minutes. Add the onion, garlic, bay leaves and orange juice. Pour in the chicken stock, cola and heavy cream. Add the bouquet garni and bring to a boil. Reduce the heat to medium-low, cover and continue to simmer until the pork is very tender, about 2½ hours.

Preheat the oven to 400°F (200°C).

Remove the pork from the Dutch oven. Place on a parchment-lined sheet pan. Drizzle with a small amount of the reserved cooking liquid and lightly season with salt.

Roast the pork in the oven until browned, about 30 minutes. Flake apart with forks or chop into small pieces. Serve on a plate with beans and rice or make some delicious tacos.

Apricot-Glazed Roast Pork Tenderloin

Pork and fruit is a classic culinary pairing. The sweet tartness of fruit is perfect with the earthy, savory taste of pork. It's widely taught that fruits and vegetables eaten by animals pair with them on the plate. This is especially true for pigs. They eat a lot of fruits, nuts and mushrooms, so those ingredients naturally go very well with pork. Tenderloin is the same muscle as filet mignon in beef. So similarly, tenderloin is tender, has little fat or connective tissue and is great for those who don't like too much fat or chew in their meat. Roasting is probably the easiest way to cook anything! Just remember roasting is 400°F (200°C) or higher. And always season and lubricate anything you're roasting!

Serves 4

2 lb (910 g) pork tenderloin

¼ cup (60 ml) extra virgin olive oil, divided

Kosher salt and pepper, to taste

3 sprigs fresh thyme, leaves stripped off, stems discarded

1 sprig rosemary, leaves stripped off, rough chopped

1 (10-oz [280-g]) jar apricot preserves

1 tbsp (15 ml) soy sauce

¼ cup (60 ml) dry sherry

1 tbsp (6 g) grated ginger

Preheat the oven to 425°F (220°C).

On a large plate, roll the tenderloins in 3 tablespoons (45 ml) of the olive oil. Season with salt, pepper, fresh thyme and chopped rosemary.

Combine the apricot preserves, soy sauce, sherry and grated ginger in a small saucepan and cook over low heat for 3 to 4 minutes. Once the preserves melt into a nice glaze, remove from the heat and reserve.

Heat a cast-iron skillet or other ovenproof sauté pan over medium-high heat. Add the remaining 1 tablespoon (15 ml) of olive oil. When the first wisp of white smoke appears, add the pork and sear until golden brown on all sides, about 8 minutes total. Brush the apricot mixture over the pork and transfer the skillet to the preheated oven. Cook for 5 minutes, then flip the pieces over, brush again with the apricot mixture and return to the oven.

Roast until the pork reaches an internal temperature of 135°F (57°C) in the thickest portion. Remove from the oven, tent loosely with foil and let rest until the internal temperature reaches 140°F (60°C) for a nice medium (8 to 10 minutes). If you want it a little more well done, remove from the oven at 140°F (60°C) and let rest until 145°F (63°C).

Slice and serve with the apricot sauce. This would be a great protein with any of the vegetable sides.

Chef Tips: You can substitute any fruit preserve in this dish. Blackberry, blueberry, raspberry and rhubarb would be delicious here.

Large pieces of meat can absorb a good amount of salt, so don't be shy when seasoning your tenderloin.

Slow Cooker Pulled Pork

We love pulled pork but never have the time to babysit and smoke a pork butt (shoulder) for half a day. We created this recipe to replicate that pull-apart, smoky, tender deliciousness. Store the pork in an airtight container in the freezer. You'll have pulled pork any time of year. Liquid smoke is very controversial in the barbecue world, similar to the way truffle oil is in the chef world. We feel in small amounts it can add the missing smoky magic when you don't have a smoker.

Serves 6–8

Pork

½ tsp liquid smoke (optional)

1 (4-lb [1.8-kg]) bone-in pork shoulder roast (or might be called blade roast or butt roast)

½ cup (80 g) Barbecue Rub (page 53)

2 large onions, sliced

8 cloves garlic, smashed

2 sprigs fresh thyme

2 bay leaves

2 sprigs fresh oregano

¼ cup (60 ml) apple cider vinegar

¾ cup (180 ml) chicken stock, homemade (page 107) or store-bought

For Finishing

¾ cup (180 g) ketchup

2 tbsp (22 g) yellow mustard

2 tbsp (30 ml) apple cider vinegar

1 tsp salt, or to taste

To make the pork, if using, rub the liquid smoke on the roast. Next, generously coat all surfaces of the pork roast with the rub mixture. Allow the roast to sit on the counter for 30 minutes.

If you have a slow cooker that has a browning function, preheat it and brown the roast in the cooker insert on all sides. If your slow cooker doesn't have browning capability, simply use a large sauté pan on the stove over medium heat. Add the onions, garlic and herbs, and cook for 5 to 10 minutes, until the onion softens and begins to color. Add the apple cider vinegar and chicken stock, heat through, then change the mode to slow cook on high for 3 hours or low for 5 hours, or until the internal temperature registers 190°F (88°C) on a meat thermometer.

To finish, remove the meat from the slow cooker and let rest until it's cool enough to handle. Discard the herb stems and bay leaves. Cut the meat into finger-size shreds and discard the excess fat. Skim off the fat from the drippings and mix in the ketchup, mustard, vinegar and salt. Don't be "skerred" to salt it—taste and adjust the seasonings. Add the liquid, as well as the onions and garlic, to the shredded meat, which will soak up some of the juice. Use while warm or let cool and refrigerate or freeze until needed.

> **Chef Tips:** Pork butt isn't what you think. It's actually the shoulder. Back in colonial days, these less desirable shoulder cuts were tossed into barrels called "butts" for storage. This cut has the perfect amount of fat to lean and is super versatile. It's great for slow cooking and for quick grilling.
>
> If you have a smoker of any kind, season the meat with the rub and smoke the butt at 225 to 250°F (107 to 120°C) for about 4 hours, or until falling apart. Finish with our barbecue sauce (page 53).

SEAFOOD

Professional Hacks to Cook Flawless Fish and Seafood Dishes

I think most people find seafood difficult to cook. We think it's because a lot of them don't have enough practice with it. Most home cooks leave seafood to the restaurants and consider it a special-occasion food. Seafood is also more expensive per pound. So, few want to take the risk and potentially blow a bunch of cash on experimenting.

A good rule for selecting seafood is to use all your senses. Look for a translucent wet look on all seafood. From calamari to shrimp to fish, it all should look shiny like it's right out of the water. Dry, dark, sunken eyes and spots are obviously bad. Touch your seafood whenever you can at the market, but be gentle. Seafood should always feel firm and never yield to a gentle squeeze. Smell everything. All seafood should smell like the ocean, not like nothing. Seafood has a smell—if you like to eat it, you'll know pleasant smells from off ones.

Frozen is not a bad thing. Most seafood has been IQF frozen, which means individually quick frozen. The seafood is cleaned and immediately frozen after being harvested. The freezer is set to -40°F (-40°C) and the fish is cryogenically frozen. So by the time it's thawed at the market, the seafood is incredibly fresh. This type of freezing keeps fish fillets from forming crystals. Most sushi fish is processed this way.

There are a few fundamentals to cooking seafood regardless of which species it is. Don't overcook it. Unlike other proteins, there is no internal temperature for various seafood. All seafood cooks quickly, and the result of overcooking is the seafood becomes dry and very tough.

Dry heat is usually the best method, with a few exceptions. In this chapter, we're frying, roasting, stir-frying and sautéing. Dry heat lends itself better because it seals the exterior and cooks food quickly. The best moist heat methods for seafood are steaming, like for shellfish or fish en papillote, and boiling for stews. We're also making a ceviche, which is fish cured in lemon juice.

Never marinate seafood for more than 1 hour. Because seafood is so delicate, marinating too long will break it down and make it mealy.

Practice. The keys to working with seafood are practice and repetition. From cutting to cooking, you have to do it a lot of times to build that muscle memory.

Oven-Roasted Halibut with Sauce Gribiche

Most people love salmon, but I really think halibut is the vanilla ice cream of fish. Its mild flavor and meatiness are great for both fish lovers and folks who are undecided. Of all of the cooking methods out there, roasting is my absolute favorite for a few reasons. It's the most user-friendly, requiring the least effort by the cook. It creates a great browning (Maillard) effect. It also is the easiest to clean up. Make foil and parchment paper your friend and cleanup will be a snap! Gribiche is a classic French sauce that uses hard-boiled egg as a base to make a creamy, sophisticated sauce. It's like a very fancy tartar sauce, and I love it with fish.

Serves 4

Sauce Gribiche
3 eggs

3 tbsp (33 g) Dijon mustard

2 tbsp (30 ml) white wine vinegar

6 tbsp (90 ml) extra virgin olive oil

3–5 cornichons, cut into small dice

2 tbsp (16 g) capers

3 tbsp (12 g) chopped fresh parsley

Kosher salt and freshly ground black pepper, to taste

Fish
4 (6-oz [168-g]) halibut fillets, 1" (2.5 cm) thick

1 tbsp (15 ml) extra virgin olive oil, plus more to taste

Kosher salt and freshly ground black pepper, to taste

1 tsp paprika

4 sprigs fresh thyme

To make the sauce, for perfect hard-boiled eggs, bring a saucepan of water to a boil over high heat. Add the cold eggs and cook for 10 minutes. Shock in ice water and chill for 15 minutes. Set aside.

Place the mustard, vinegar and olive oil in a mini-prep processor. Pulse 3 to 5 times, until emulsified. Fold in the cornichons, capers and eggs, and pulse 2 more times, until the mixture is combined but still chunky and uneven. Transfer to a small bowl and stir in the parsley. Season to taste with salt and black pepper.

To make the fish, preheat the oven to 450°F (230°C). Pat the fish fillets dry with a paper towel and place the fish in a baking dish sprayed with oil. Drizzle with the olive oil and season with the salt, pepper and paprika. Top each fillet with a thyme sprig.

Bake until just opaque, about 10 minutes. For more color, place the pan under the broiler for 1 to 2 minutes. Drizzle the sauce on each fillet and serve.

> **Chef Tip:** Gribiche is classically paired with seafood, vegetables and game meats, but we also love to use it as a spread for sandwiches and wraps or as a dip for crudités.

Garlicky Lemony Shrimp Scampi

An Italian–American classic, these garlicky and wine-bathed beauties can be prepared quickly in your kitchen. Many cooks serve them over pasta or with a side of crusty bread, and either would make a great meal. Don't skimp on the shrimp size: use at least 21–25 (shrimp per pound [454 g]) or even jumbos (10–15 shrimp per pound [454 g]) because small shrimp cook too fast and don't have that plump, crisp texture. The key to this dish is to get that pan smoking hot before you start and to work fast. Mise en place is important, so have all your items prepped to keep up with the speed of the heat.

Serves 4

2 tbsp (28 g) unsalted butter

2 tbsp (30 ml) extra virgin olive oil

4 cloves garlic, minced

½ cup (120 ml) dry white wine or chicken stock

Heavy pinch of Maldon salt

Pinch of crushed red pepper flakes (optional)

Freshly ground black pepper

2 lb (910 g) large or extra-large shrimp, peeled and deveined

¼ cup (60 ml) freshly squeezed lemon juice

2 tbsp (8 g) chopped fresh Italian parsley

Heat a large skillet over high heat for 1 to 2 minutes. You want the pan hot but not smoking hot; you can add a few drops of water to see if they sear and evaporate immediately. Swirl in the butter and olive oil until the butter melts and the pan smokes lightly. Toss in the garlic and sauté for about 30 seconds, or until fragrant. Carefully pour in the wine and cook, swirling, until reduced by half, 30 seconds to 1 minute. Season with salt, red pepper flakes and black pepper.

Add the shrimp, constantly tossing until they just turn from translucent to slightly opaque or pink, 2 to 4 minutes depending on the size. Add the lemon juice and parley. Remove from the heat and serve immediately.

> **Chef Tip:** If serving with pasta, be sure to cook the pasta first before making the shrimp. If serving with bread, I like to slice the crusty bread super thick, or 3 to 4 inches (7.5 to 10 cm). Drizzle with olive oil and grill on high until golden brown but soft in the middle.

Seared Sea Scallops with Fresh Fava Bean Purée

Perfectly seared scallops is one of those benchmarks that all cooks strive for. Here are a few tips to help you master these mollusks. First, always buy scallops that are firm and cold. They should bounce back like a firm steak. They should look moist, almost oily, and smell like the beach. Moisture is the enemy of browning, so be sure to pat your scallops dry before cooking. Pan selection is also key. Cast iron or steel is best because it retains heat amazingly well; this will cauterize and sear the scallop instead of boiling the moisture out of them, making them tough.

Serves 4

Fresh Fava Bean Purée
1 lb (454 g) packaged steamed fava beans

2 tbsp (30 ml) chicken stock, homemade (page 107) or low-sodium canned

¼ cup (60 ml) heavy cream, or more as needed

1 tsp kosher salt

Freshly ground pepper, to taste

Scallops
2 tsp (10 ml) olive oil

8 sea scallops, U10 or larger

Salt and freshly ground pepper, to taste

Freshly squeezed lemon juice, to taste

1 tbsp (4 g) coarsely chopped Italian parsley

To make the purée, place the peeled and steamed fava beans in a food processor. Add the stock, cream, salt and pepper and process until smooth and creamy, a few pulses at a time, about 1 minute. If not creamy enough, add a tablespoon (15 ml) of cream at a time until smooth. The purée should feel like creamy mashed potatoes. Scrape into a saucepan and warm gently over low heat for about 2 minutes. You can hold it warm until the scallops are ready.

To make the scallops, heat a 12- to 14-inch (30.5 to 35.5-cm) cast-iron skillet over high heat for 2 to 3 minutes. Reduce the heat to medium-high and add the olive oil. Pat the scallops dry with a clean paper towel and season with salt and pepper. Carefully place the scallops in the hot skillet. Let them sear, without disturbing them, until browned, 1 to 2 minutes. Turn and cook for about 1 more minute, until warm in the middle. Transfer the scallops to a paper towel–lined plate and let rest. Sprinkle with lemon juice.

Mound about ½ cup (120 g) of fava bean purée onto the centers of 4 plates. Top with 2 scallops each, sprinkle with the parsley and serve immediately.

> **Chef Tip**: Look for scallops that are U10 or larger (the "U" means "under"). So U10 means under 10 per pound (454 g). The lower the U number, the larger the scallop.

Fried Fish Tacos with Chipotle Crema

This fast and easy fish taco dish will be an instant classic in your house. You can use just about any fish that you love, from catfish to rock fish, for this recipe. It's also a great way to use smaller fish that don't yield perfect fillets. If you prefer crispy fried fish tacos, use the dredge, batter and fry technique from the Better-Than-Takeout Orange Chicken recipe (page 46) for the fish.

Serves 4

Chipotle Crema

¼ cup (60 g) mayonnaise

½ cup (120 g) sour cream

2 limes, 1 halved and juiced, 1 cut into wedges

Kosher salt and freshly ground black pepper, to taste

1 tbsp (8 g) finely chopped canned chipotle pepper, plus 1 tbsp (15 ml) adobo sauce (optional)

Fish Tacos

6 tbsp (90 ml) vegetable oil, divided

8 (6" [15-cm]) corn tortillas

1 lb (454 g) flounder fillet or any firm white-fleshed fish, skinless and boneless, cut across the grain of the flesh into strips about ½" wide x 3" long (1.3 x 7.5 cm)

Kosher salt and freshly ground black pepper, to taste

1½ tsp (4 g) chili powder

1 tbsp (14 g) unsalted butter

Pico de Gallo (page 72), for serving

Guacamole (page 73), for serving

2 cups (140 g) shredded green cabbage, rinsed in ice water and dried well

Mexican hot sauce, such as Tapatio, Cholula or Valentina, for serving

To make the chipotle crema, in a small bowl, whisk the mayonnaise and sour cream until combined. Season to taste with lime juice, salt, pepper and chipotle (if using).

To make the fish tacos, pour 2 tablespoons (30 ml) of the oil into a small bowl. Separate the corn tortillas from each other, but keep them in a stack and run the outside edges through the oil. Heat them in a dry skillet a few at a time, until they are soft and hot. Keep them warm, wrapped in a clean, dry dish towel or a tortilla warmer, if available.

Season the fish with salt, pepper and the chili powder. Warm a plate and line it with paper towels.

Pour the remaining ¼ cup (60 ml) of vegetable oil into a 12-inch (30.5-cm) frying pan and place over medium-high heat until it shimmers and is about to smoke. Add the butter to the pan. Place some fish pieces in the oil, without crowding them, and cook until deep golden brown on one side, 2 to 3 minutes. Turn carefully and cook for 1 minute more. Remove to the warmed, paper towel–lined plate and sprinkle with salt. Repeat with the remaining fish.

Fill each tortilla with 3 pieces of fish, browned-side up, followed by pico de gallo, guacamole and a bit of cabbage. Drizzle with the crema. Serve 2 tacos per person, with lime wedges and hot sauce on the side.

Chef Tip: Chipotle chiles are simply smoked jalapeño peppers. They are cooked in liquid with tomato added to make the famous canned chipotles in adobo. The sauce from those canned chiles is called adobo.

Pico de Gallo

All cooks need to know how to make pico de gallo. Stop buying premade salsas. Once you learn how to make this pico, you can make any salsa, including popular fruit salsas. It's also a great recipe to make while developing your knife skills. Try to get all the cuts consistent and straight. Use a serrated knife for the tomatoes and a chef's knife for everything else. Another knife-related skill is turning the garlic into a paste. First chop it up small, then take the salt used in the recipe and carefully press it into the garlic with the side of the knife.

Makes 3 cups (675 g)

1 lb (454 g) fresh tomatoes, cored and cut into medium dice

¾ cup (120 g) minced white onion

1 clove garlic, minced

Juice of 1 lime (about 2 tbsp [30 ml])

½ tsp kosher salt

⅛ tsp black pepper

1 jalapeño or other hot fresh chile, stemmed, seeded and minced, or cayenne or crushed red pepper flakes to taste

½ cup (20 g) chopped cilantro, or to taste

In a small bowl, combine all the ingredients except the cilantro, and taste. Add more salt, pepper or chiles if desired. Stir in half the cilantro and set aside for 30 to 60 minutes. Adjust the seasoning, garnish with the remaining cilantro and serve.

If the tomatoes are lacking flavor, try boosting it with ½ teaspoon granulated or raw sugar.

If milder salsa is desired, reduce or omit the jalapeño. If spicier salsa is desired, the seeds can be left in, as well as the amount increased overall. If you're not sure, try putting in half the amount called for, then adding according to your taste. It's safer than adding too much in one go.

Guacamole

Make real guacamole and stop buying it from the store; there is nothing easier and more delicious. "Avocado pulp" from the store isn't from ripe fruit and is full of preservatives that make it taste tinny and its never really creamy. This dish is an essential for every cook and it's not just for chips. I use it as a spread instead of mayonnaise and a dip for crudités for the kids. I believe in simplicity for guacamole, but you can get fancy and add anything to this recipe, such as tomato, mango and even chile, to make your guacamole more interesting.

Makes 2 cups (450 g)

2 ripe Hass avocados
¼ cup (40 g) minced onion
1 serrano pepper, finely minced
1 tbsp (3 g) minced cilantro
1 tsp garlic salt
1 tbsp (15 ml) lime juice
Salt and pepper, to taste

Slice the avocados in half around the pit. Stick your knife into the pit and twist to remove. Scoop the avocado flesh into a medium-size bowl. Mash the avocado with a fork until there are no lumps. Stir in the onion, serrano pepper, cilantro, garlic salt and lime juice.

Add salt and pepper to taste. Cover and refrigerate until serving.

Crispy-Skin Salmon with Lemon-Caper Yogurt Sauce

One of the most prestigious stations in a classic brigade kitchen is the fish station. The fish cook or chef is called the poissonnier. A true test of the poissonnier is how crispy the skin is and getting that fish perfectly cooked, which means moist but still flaky. The technique of scraping the skin to remove moisture and crisp the skin can be applied to all fish. The lemon-caper sauce is luscious and briny, perfect for fish. I also love serving this sauce with fried seafood dishes like calamari (page 79), shrimp or fish and chips.

Serves 4

4 (6-oz [168-g]) salmon fillets, skin on, scales and pin bones removed

Salt and freshly ground pepper, to taste

3 tbsp (45 ml) extra virgin olive oil

Lemon-Caper Yogurt Sauce

¼ cup (15 g) chopped fresh parsley

2 tbsp (16 g) capers, minced

2 anchovy fillets, minced

2 cloves garlic, minced

2 tbsp (22 g) whole-grain Dijon mustard

Grated zest of 1 lemon

2 tbsp (30 ml) freshly squeezed lemon juice

½ cup (120 g) whole-milk Greek yogurt

2 tbsp (30 ml) extra virgin olive oil

Pat the salmon dry with paper towels. With the sharp edge of a knife, scrape the skin back and forth the length of the fillet over and over with light pressure. You will see moisture build up on your knife edge; wipe it away. Continue for about 1 minute, until there's almost nothing to wipe away. Season the salmon with salt and pepper on both sides. Drizzle with the olive oil and set aside until ready to cook.

To make the sauce, in a bowl, combine all the ingredients with a fork until well mixed. Taste, and then season as necessary. Set aside.

Heat a cast-iron skillet over medium-high heat for 3 to 4 minutes. There is no need to oil the pan, because you oiled the fish. Start the salmon skin-side down, laying them away from you. Cook for about 3 minutes, or until golden brown. Shake the pan until the salmon lifts and moves by itself.

Carefully turn the salmon pieces over and reduce the heat to medium-low (to cook the flesh more slowly). The thin pieces will be done quicker than the thick ones, so be ready to take those out first. Cook for another 2 to 3 minutes, or until the salmon just slightly resists when pierced with a thin-bladed knife, or registers 115°F (46°C) in the thickest part for medium-rare, or 125°F (52°C) for medium but still juicy.

Plate the salmon fillets and top with the sauce right before you eat to keep the skin nice and crispy.

> **Chef Tip:** Buy a fish spatula (also known as a fish turner). It's very thin and flexible, perfect for getting under fillets without tearing or breaking the fish.

Rock Fish Ceviche Tostadas

I grew up working on fishing boats and have been making this ceviche recipe for over twenty years. It's a great way to change up your fish game. Ceviche is not raw fish; it's actually "cooked" by the acid of limes or lemons. You can make ceviche from any fish, but it tastes best with leaner, white-meat fish. I like to make it with West Coast barracuda, sculpin, snapper and halibut.

Makes 4 tostadas

1 lb (454 g) firm white-fleshed ocean fish, like snapper or halibut

Kosher salt

½ cup (120 ml) plus 2 tbsp (30 ml) freshly squeezed lime juice, divided

¼ cup (40 g) finely diced red onion

¼ cup (25 g) chopped scallion

2 medium ripe tomatoes, cut into small dice

2 tsp (6 g) thinly sliced serrano chile

4 corn tostadas or 12–16 large tortilla chips

½ cup (20 g) roughly chopped fresh cilantro

2 firm ripe avocados, pitted, peeled and thinly sliced

Mexican hot sauce, such as Cholula or Tapatio

Lime wedges, for serving

Cut the fish into small dice, place in a glass bowl and sprinkle with salt. Add ½ cup (120 ml) of the lime juice and mix well. Cover with plastic wrap, pressing down so the fish is submerged in the juice. Refrigerate for 45 minutes, or up to 2 hours for a firmer texture.

Drain the fish in a colander and return it to the mixing bowl. Stir in the onion, scallion, tomatoes, remaining 2 tablespoons (30 ml) of lime juice and half the chile. Taste and season with salt if necessary.

Place the tostada on a large plate and spoon the ceviche mixture on top. Garnish with the cilantro, remaining chile, avocado and a few drops of Mexican hot sauce. Serve with lime wedges.

> **Chef Tip:** You can make ceviche in less than 30 minutes if you have a vacuum sealer by placing the citrus-marinated fish in a vacuum bag. Pulling the oxygen out of the bag pulls the citrus into the fish and speeds the process.

Light and Crispy Calamari with Fried Lemons

Calamari is one of our favorite seafood dishes. They are crispy light bites of ocean candy and teach the essential technique of a quick dredge and deep-fry. It's very similar to fried chicken with a soak in dairy, which does a few important things. It sweetens the taste of fresh seafood by sucking out the strong ocean flavors that some don't like. It also creates the base of the crunchy batter by clinging to the cornmeal to make a phenomenal crust. And also like fried chicken, you can double dredge by running the crust through the cream, flour and cornmeal a second time. This technique also works with fish sticks, clams, oysters and cuttlefish. It's basically great for small bits of meat or seafood that need a crispy crust. Pair this with tomato sauce (page 37) or some tartar sauce for a great starter or snack.

Makes 4 appetizer portions

Calamari

1 (1½-lb [680-g]) whole squid or 1 (12-oz [340-g]) package cleaned squid

2 cups (480 ml) heavy cream

2 eggs

Salt and freshly ground pepper, to taste

½ onion, thinly sliced on a mandoline

½ lemon, very thinly sliced

Dredge Mix

2 cups (240 g) all-purpose flour

¾ cup (90 g) cornstarch

½ cup (75 g) cornmeal

1 tsp mild paprika

Salt and freshly ground pepper, to taste

2 qt (1.8 L) oil, for frying

Chopped fresh parsley, for garnish

1 tbsp (6 g) grated lemon zest

Easy Homemade Tomato Sauce (page 37), warmed, for dipping

To make the calamari, clean the squid. To clean a whole squid, separate the head and tentacles from the body. With a paring knife, cut between the eyes and the tentacles, discarding the eye portion. In the center of the tentacles, push out a little round bead with the hard beak and discard it; reserve the tentacles. For the body section, peel off the flaps and the dark-colored membrane. Remove the quill, the plastic-like bone. Squeeze out the innards like squeezing out toothpaste. Rinse the tentacles and body sections and dry well. Cut the body sections into nice rings. Leave the legs intact.

Whisk the heavy cream and eggs together in a medium-size bowl and season with salt and pepper. Soak the squid, onion and lemon for 45 minutes to 1 hour.

To make the dredge mix, combine the flour, cornstarch, cornmeal, paprika, salt and pepper in a separate bowl.

Pour the oil into a heavy 5-quart (4.5-L) Dutch oven or any heavy-bottomed pot at least twice as deep as the oil and heat to 365°F (185°C) on a frying thermometer. Keep the lid nearby in case of emergency.

Drain the squid, onion and lemon, leaving some cream stuck to them, then immediately place in the bowl of flour. Roll everything around so the flour mix sticks to the cream like a heavy dredge. Knock off any excess. Fry in small batches until crispy and golden brown, about 1 minute. Drain well on paper towels or a rack and season again with a little salt and pepper.

Garnish with the chopped parsley and lemon zest, and serve with the tomato sauce.

> **Chef Tip:** If you can't find squid, cuttlefish is readily available at the fishmonger. They are squiddy cousins that grow large and are very meaty.

RICE, PASTA AND PIZZA

Classic Grain-Based Dishes Every Cook Needs

We grouped rice, pasta and pizza together because they are grain based. Rice and wheat are ancient relatives that were domesticated by humans and eaten for thousands of years. From the modern cook's perspective, we purchase grains in two forms, flour or whole. Wheat contains gluten, unlike rice.

Although we associate pasta with Italian cuisine, a lot of food historians believe it was brought to Italy in the thirteenth century by Marco Polo. Pasta made its way to the Americas with early Spanish settlers. Pasta and noodles can be made with many different grains, including durum and semolina, and even blends. Because of the more recent awareness of gluten allergies and the general trend of being gluten free, there are a lot of gluten-free pastas on the market.

The key with pasta is not to overcook it and be thoughtful about how you're going to use it. If you know you're going to be boiling pasta or noodles and then adding sauce, it's a good idea to undercook it and account for the hot sauce cooking it again.

A note on flour for making your own pizza dough and breads: most store-bought all-purpose flour contains 10 to 13 percent protein. Bread flour has 14 to 16 percent protein and cake flour has 7 to 8 percent. Protein content in flour dictates its ability to form gluten. Gluten in flour is what makes the stretchiness in dough. You want higher-protein flour for breads that need chew and lower-protein flour for items like biscuits that are airy and flaky. Pizza should be made with all-purpose or bread flour, which has more protein.

Not-as-Hard-as-You-Think Risotto

Risotto is one of those dishes that all cooks fear but really shouldn't. The beauty of the dish is it feels and eats like it has a ton of cream and cheese, but it doesn't. When you cook down that starchy Arborio rice nice and slowly, it gelatinizes and feels creamy! You can finish it with a little butter and cheese, but the rice and cooking process are what give it that luxurious deliciousness. You can play with different stocks and ingredients to make your risotto fun and interesting.

Serves 4

6 cups (1.4 L) low-sodium vegetable broth

2 tbsp (28 g) unsalted butter, divided

2 tbsp (30 ml) olive oil

1½ cups (300 g) Arborio rice

½ cup (80 g) finely chopped onion about the size of rice grains

1 clove garlic, minced

½ tsp kosher salt, divided

½ cup (120 ml) white wine

1 cup (100 g) grated pecorino cheese

¼ tsp freshly ground white pepper, or to taste

½ cup (12 g) fresh basil leaves

Place the broth in a medium-size saucepan and bring to a low simmer over medium heat. While the broth heats, place a wide saucepan over medium-low heat and add 1 tablespoon (14 g) of the butter and the olive oil. When the butter has melted, add the rice and sauté until aromatic, about 1 minute. Then add the onion, garlic and ¼ teaspoon of the salt. Continue stirring until the onion is soft and translucent without becoming brown, about 3 minutes.

Raise the heat to medium and add the wine to the rice mixture. Stir until the wine is absorbed, 2 to 3 minutes. Begin adding the hot broth one ladle at a time, stirring constantly and allowing each ladle of broth to be absorbed before adding the next. Cook the rice until al dente (tender but slightly chewy), about 20 minutes. If you use up all the hot broth and the rice isn't quite there, change to hot water.

Remove the pan from the heat and add the pecorino, remaining tablespoon (14 g) of butter and remaining ¼ teaspoon of salt, mixing well. Season with white pepper to taste and transfer to a large platter. Scatter with the basil leaves and serve immediately.

> **Chef Tips:** Cream should never be added to risotto. The "sauce" comes from the proper creaming of the rice grains made by stirring the stock and the cheese. Butter is allowed and encouraged.
>
> Some of our favorite add-ins are mushroom stock and mushrooms, and asparagus, peas and saffron.
>
> The texture of risotto should be *all'onda*, "wavy, flowing like waves." Traditionally served on plates, risotto should lie flat on the plate and not pile up. It should not have any excess liquid sweating off the rice.

Perfect Jasmine Rice

This is another fundamental recipe from my first book and I wanted to make sure you have it in case you don't have that book. It's not sexy, not one to impress your friends. But you will find yourself making this recipe over and over again during your lifetime. This finger measurement works for all long-grain white rice varieties, including basmati, American white rice and white rice hybrids like Texmati. Trying to cook rice with static formulas like 1 cup (190 g) of rice to 1½ cups (355 ml) of water is a recipe for disaster because the more rice you cook, the less water you need. So just remember to measure water to the first crease in your index finger and you'll have perfect rice every time.

Serves 2–4

1¼ cups (237 g) long-grain jasmine rice

1¾ cups (415 ml) water

Add the rice to a fine-mesh strainer and rinse under cold running water while swirling with your fingers to wash the rice. Wash the rice for about 30 seconds and then rinse for about a minute.

Add the rice to a 2-quart (1.8-L) saucepan. Insert your index finger until touching the top of the rice with your fingertip. Add water until the water just reaches the first crease of your finger. Turn the heat to high. As soon as the water reaches a boil, give everything a good stir, reduce the heat to a low simmer and cover the pot. After 20 minutes, remove the pot from the heat and let it sit for at least 15 minutes before fluffing with a fork and serving.

Arroz con Pollo

It's important to have a few one-pot meals in your repertoire that can be cooked within an hour. Arroz con pollo is a Spanish dish that has regional variations from different countries. The distinct yellow-orange color comes from an ingredient called annatto. Annatto powder is ground from the seeds of the achiote tree. It creates a saffron-like color but is very inexpensive. It's a great ingredient for any cook to know. You can find it at Asian and Latin markets as well as on the Internet.

Serves 2–4

1 tbsp (15 ml) olive oil

½ whole chicken, cut into 4 pieces

Salt and freshly ground pepper, to taste

3 cloves garlic, minced

1 small onion, thinly sliced

1 cup (150 g) chopped green bell pepper

2 cups (380 g) uncooked long-grain white rice

½ cup (120 ml) Easy Homemade Tomato Sauce (page 37)

2½ cups (600 ml) chicken stock, homemade (page 107) or store-bought

½ tsp annatto powder

1 bay leaf

¼ tsp ground cumin

Heat a Dutch oven over medium-high heat for 1 minute. Add the oil and tilt to coat the bottom. Pat the chicken pieces dry with a paper towel. Season well with salt and pepper. Sear the chicken pieces in the oil, turning every minute until just browned on all sides, about 5 minutes.

Stir in the garlic, onion and bell pepper and sauté until translucent, about 2 minutes. Stir in the rice and toast, stirring, for about 1 minute. Stir in the tomato sauce, chicken stock, annatto powder, bay leaf and cumin. Season generously with salt and a pinch of pepper.

Cover and simmer over low heat for 20 minutes, until the water is absorbed and the rice is cooked through. Let rest for about 10 minutes before fluffing and serving.

> **Chef Tips:** You can also finish your arroz con pollo in the oven. Once all the seasonings and stock are in, just pop it into a 350°F (180°C) oven for 1 hour.
>
> You can substitute a few threads of saffron for the annatto powder.

Wild Rice with Almonds and Dried Cranberries

Wild rice isn't actually rice; it's an aquatic grass that grows wild in different parts of the world, including the U.S. Great Lakes region. There is even one type in Texas that's in danger of going extinct. Wild rice is higher in protein and nutrients than real rice. It's an heirloom food that we want to shine a light on. So buy it, cook it and enjoy it. It's one of the few heirloom foods that is native to the United States.

Serves 6–8

¼ cup (56 g) butter

1½ large onions, chopped

3 cloves garlic, minced

5 cups (1.2 L) canned low-salt chicken stock

1 cup (160 g) wild rice

1½ cups (270 g) long-grain brown rice

1½ cups (180 g) dried cranberries

¼ cup (15 g) chopped fresh parsley

2 sprigs fresh thyme, leaves stripped from stems, chopped

1¼ cups (138 g) slivered almonds

¾ cup (75 g) chopped scallions

1 tsp kosher salt, or to taste

½ tsp ground black pepper, or to taste

Melt the butter in a large, heavy pot over medium-high heat. Add the onions and garlic and sauté until tender, about 4 minutes. Add the chicken stock and bring to a boil. Add the wild rice. Reduce the heat to medium-low. Cover and simmer for 30 minutes. Mix in the brown rice; cover and simmer until the rice is just tender and most liquid is absorbed, about 30 minutes longer.

Stir the cranberries, parsley and thyme into the rice mixture. Cover and continue cooking until the liquid is absorbed, about 5 minutes longer. Mix in the almonds and scallions. Season generously with salt and pepper.

> **Chef Tip:** You can use this dish as a simple stuffing or dressing. It's great paired with duck, turkey, pork or venison. We love to make this recipe for the holidays.

Classic Spaghetti Carbonara

Carbonara is a simple and super satisfying dish you can cook in less than 30 minutes. It's also high in the chef cred category. It's a beautifully choreographed dance of rendering, boiling and finishing and a universally loved dish by old and young. I love cooking dry pasta just a little less than the box says. I always pull it about 30 seconds earlier than the directions to make sure I have al dente pasta. And I pull it 1 minute earlier if the pasta is going to keep cooking in a sauce for a few minutes.

Serves 4

2 large eggs, at room temperature

3 large egg yolks, at room temperature

½ cup (50 g) grated Pecorino Romano

¾ cup (75 g) grated Parmesan, divided

Salt and freshly ground pepper, to taste

1 tbsp (15 ml) olive oil

4 oz (112 g) pancetta, sliced into thin rectangles about ½'' x ¾'' (1.3 x 2 cm)

1 (1-lb [454-g]) box dried spaghetti

In a small mixing bowl, whisk together the eggs, yolks, Pecorino and ½ cup (50 g) of the Parmesan. Season with a pinch of salt and a generous pinch of pepper.

In a large skillet over medium-high heat, heat the oil and add the pancetta. Cook for 3 to 5 minutes, until the fat renders and the pancetta is crispy. Remove from the heat.

Bring a large pot of water to a boil over high heat, then add the pasta and about 1 tablespoon (18 g) of salt and cook the pasta according to the package instructions. Pull the pasta from the heat about 30 seconds earlier than the package says. Remove about 1 cup (235 ml) of hot pasta water before draining the spaghetti in a colander.

Just before the pasta is cooked, reheat the pancetta in the skillet over low heat. Dump in the pasta. Stir in the egg and cheese mixture and add half the reserved pasta water. Stir it all well until creamy. Taste and season if necessary. Stir in more pasta water if you want the dish saucier. Top with the remaining ¼ cup (25 g) of Parmesan and serve immediately.

Chef Tip: NEVER rinse your pasta after cooking! You need the pasta grippy, so sauces and seasonings will stick to it.

Mornay Sauce Mac and Cheese

There are five foundational sauces in French cooking, aka the French mother sauces: béchamel, velouté, espagnole, tomato and hollandaise. Béchamel is the one that makes a creamy-style sauce. It starts with a roux, which is a mixture of flour and butter cooked over heat. Then you add milk to that magical mixture, and you get a basic cream sauce. Melt cheese into the béchamel and you've created a Mornay sauce. The flour and butter bind to the cheese and distribute it into the milk to stabilize it. If you just melted cheese in a pot, it would clump and break. This cheese sauce is great for dipping but also perfect for making mac and cheese.

Serves 4

1 (1-lb [454-g]) box dried elbow macaroni

3 tbsp (42 g) unsalted butter

¼ cup (30 g) all-purpose flour

4 cups (960 ml) cold whole milk

½ cup (60 g) finely grated Gruyère cheese

2⅓ cups (265 g) finely grated cheddar cheese

½ cup (50 g) finely grated Parmigiano-Reggiano cheese

Coarse salt, to taste

Pinch of white pepper

⅛ tsp freshly ground nutmeg

Bring a large pot of water to a boil over high heat, add the pasta and about 1 tablespoon (18 g) of salt and cook according to the package instructions. Transfer to a colander and drain well.

Melt the butter in a 4-quart (3.6-L) pot over medium heat. Whisk in the flour and stir with a wooden spoon until the roux is an even gold color, about 1 minute. Stir in the cold milk and combine well. Bring to a simmer, constantly stirring, until thickened and smooth. Reduce the heat to a simmer and cook for 15 minutes.

Add the cheeses, stirring constantly until completely melted and the sauce is smooth. Season with the salt, white pepper and nutmeg. In a large serving bowl, stir the sauce and pasta together until well combined. Serve warm.

Chef Tips: You can use any dried pasta shape that you like for this recipe. Or just leave out the pasta and you have a beautiful Mornay sauce for any use.

You also have a choice when it comes to cheese. Gruyère and Parmigiano-Reggiano are sharp and nutty, and cheddar melts smooth and gives a great color. But feel free to experiment with other cheeses you love.

Basil and Pine Nut Pesto Pasta with Sun-Dried Tomatoes

Pesto is a great tool for chefs! This herbaceous, rich sauce is versatile and can do a lot of jobs. Besides being a sauce for pasta, it's great for topping meats and fish and as a spread for sandwiches and wraps. And every cook needs those dishes that are quick to cook but have a high perception of cheffiness! Pasta is always a winner because you usually can be eating within 30 minutes. Pasta cooks in less than 10 minutes, and with some strategic shopping and pantry items, you'll have a great dish.

Serves 4

Pine Nut Pesto
2 cups (50 g) fresh basil leaves

2 tbsp (18 g) pine nuts

2 large cloves garlic

½ cup (120 ml) extra virgin olive oil

½ cup (50 g) freshly grated Parmesan cheese

Salt and pepper, to taste

Pasta
1 (1-lb [454-g]) package bow-tie pasta

2 tsp (10 ml) extra virgin olive oil

2 cloves garlic, minced

½ cup (55 g) oil-packed sun-dried tomatoes, drained and cut into strips

1 cup (115 g) small fresh mozzarella balls (bocconcini)

½ cup (120 g) Pine Nut Pesto (recipe above)

Salt and freshly ground pepper, to taste

1 tbsp (4 g) crushed red pepper flakes, to taste (optional)

To make the pesto, combine the basil leaves, pine nuts and garlic in a food processor. Pulse 4 to 6 times, until very finely minced. With the machine running, slowly drizzle in the oil and process until the mixture is smooth, about 30 seconds. Add the cheese and pulse a few times until just combined. Taste and season with salt and pepper as needed. Set aside.

To make the pasta, bring a large pot of lightly salted water to a boil. Add the pasta and cook for 8 to 10 minutes, or until al dente. Drain and reserve.

Heat the oil in a large skillet over medium heat. Add the garlic and sauté until translucent, about 1 minute. Remove from the heat. Fold in the pasta, sun-dried tomatoes, mozzarella balls and ½ cup (120 g) of pesto. Continue folding to coat evenly.

Taste and season with salt and pepper as needed. For a hint of heat, add red pepper flakes, if desired.

Chef Tips: Feel free to substitute your favorite pasta in this dish. Adding some grilled chicken or steak will make it a full and complete meal.

Pesto is traditionally made with pine nuts, basil and cheese, but you can get as creative as you want. Walnuts and pistachios are great and subbing the basil for any herb or green like arugula or parsley is delicious, too. You can go old school and just chop all the pesto ingredients by hand and then fold them into the olive oil. If you need a smoother pesto for paninis or sandwiches, use a blender.

Perfect-Every-Time Pizza Dough and Pepperoni Pizza

Homemade pizza should be a staple recipe for every cook, and it's really easy to make. Not only that, but it's a great recipe to get friends and family involved. I like making the dough and shaping it into balls ahead of time. You can use them right away or even freeze them for the future. This dough also works for making calzones, dinner rolls and flatbreads.

Makes two 8–10" (20–25-cm) pizzas

Pizza Dough

1 cup (235 ml) warm water (100°F [38°C])

1 tsp active dry yeast

½ tsp extra virgin olive oil

2 tsp (12 g) kosher salt

¾ cup (90 g) bread flour or Italian 00 flour

1½ cups (180 g) all-purpose flour

Pepperoni Pizza

All-purpose flour or cornmeal, for dusting

½ cup (120 ml) Easy Homemade Tomato Sauce (page 37), divided

Drizzle of extra virgin olive oil

2 cups (230 g) shredded low-moisture mozzarella cheese, divided

16–24 slices pepperoni, divided

¼ cup (25 g) shaved Parmesan cheese, divided

2 tbsp (6 g) dried oregano, divided

To make the dough, in a large bowl, stir together the warm water, yeast, olive oil and salt until the salt dissolves. Let this mixture rest for about 10 to 20 minutes, until slightly foamy.

Transfer the yeast and water mixture to the bowl of a stand mixer, making sure to scrape all the yeast into the bowl. Add the flours to the mixing bowl. Attach a dough hook and knead on medium speed for about 4 minutes. The mixture will come together into a ball that pulls away from the sides.

Transfer the dough ball to a clean area to knead. Flour the station and knead well for about 2 minutes. Cut the ball in half and shape each into round balls. Place each ball in a lightly oiled bowl, cover with plastic and let rise in the fridge overnight. This overnight fermentation will give the dough a pleasant sourness. You can do this on the counter in an hour or two, but you won't have the same flavor from a slow rise.

To make the pizza, place a pizza steel or stone on the middle rack of the oven and preheat to its highest setting. Let the oven heat up for at least 45 minutes.

Dust the surface of a pizza peel or the back of a half sheet pan with flour or cornmeal. Stretch one ball of dough out into a 12-inch (30.5-cm) round and place on the peel or sheet pan. Place half the sauce in the center of the stretched dough and spread it out evenly with a spoon. You want to cover all but ½ inch (1.3 cm) of the edge.

Drizzle the pizza with a tiny bit of olive oil. Rain half the mozzarella over the pizza. Place half the pepperoni on the pizza in an even pattern. Sprinkle with half the Parmesan and half the dried oregano.

Slide the pizza onto the heated steel or stone in the oven. Bake until the crust is golden brown and the cheese is bubbling, 4 to 8 minutes. Remove from the heat and let rest for 2 to 5 minutes before slicing and serving. Meanwhile, repeat with the remaining dough ball and pizza ingredients to make a second pizza.

> **Chef Tip:** Baking is precise, but don't let that scare you—precise doesn't mean difficult. The trick is to weigh all your ingredients with a scale. Buy a scale that can weigh in grams.

SALAD AND SOUP

Traditional Favorites and A Few Chef Specials You Have to Try

In culinary school, some of the first things you learn are soups, salads and dressings. You will usually learn them after learning knife skills. Soups are perfect for utilizing all your cut-up vegetables and trim. They are a foundational part of cooking. Soups, salads and dressings will teach you skills such as making vinaigrettes and emulsions, sautéing, boiling and more.

Here, you'll learn how to make some classic salad dressings that are emulsions. One of the most famous emulsions is mayonnaise, and there are a ton of different sauces and dressings based on mayonnaise.

You will also learn how to make two different types of chicken stock. And you'll learn how to make roux, then learn some roux derivatives. For instance, when you add milk or cream to roux, you get béchamel. When you add stock to roux, you get velouté and also a gravy. You will also learn how to purée soup and make a chowder.

This chapter will give you a lot of tools that will appear time and again in your cooking. So enjoy, practice and don't be scared to play around and make your own variations of the recipes.

Romaine Wedge Salad with Sieved Egg

We still order old-school wedge salads regularly when we eat out. It's a classic that all cooks should know. The combination of cool crispy lettuce, smoky bacon, tangy blue cheese and tomatoes is kinda perfect. We wanted to do it one better by adding a little more protein and a lot of fun. This technique of sieved egg is like making egg snow. Pushing the egg through a sieve makes these tiny little fingers of creamy egg. It will add another dimension to any salad.

Serves 4

Blue Cheese Dressing
4 oz (112 g) mild blue cheese (see Chef Tip)

½ cup (120 ml) buttermilk

½ cup (120 g) sour cream

¼ cup (60 g) mayonnaise

4 tsp (20 ml) white wine vinegar

1 tsp sugar

¼ tsp garlic powder

Salt and freshly ground black pepper, to taste

Salad
1 large head iceberg lettuce

8 strips thick-cut applewood double-smoked bacon

4 oz (112 g) Danish blue cheese, crumbled

1 cup (150 g) grape tomatoes, sliced in half

2 large eggs, hard-boiled, peeled, white separated from yolks

¼ cup (15 g) roughly chopped fresh parsley

To make the dressing, in a small bowl, mash the blue cheese and buttermilk together with a fork until the mixture resembles large-curd cottage cheese. Stir in the sour cream, mayonnaise, vinegar, sugar and garlic powder until well blended. Season to taste with salt and pepper. Chill in the refrigerator until ready to serve.

To make the salad, prepare the lettuce by cutting out the core and portioning the lettuce into 8 wedges. Keep it cold in the refrigerator under moist paper towels until needed. Chill 4 plates in the refrigerator until ready to serve.

Prepare the bacon in the oven, on a rack, as directed on page 54. Keep the slices whole and flat.

Put the iceberg wedges onto the chilled plates, 2 slim wedges per person. Drizzle with the blue cheese dressing, garnish with 2 strips of bacon per person and add the blue cheese crumbles and grape tomatoes.

Hold a small sieve over the salad and press the hard-boiled yolks through, extruding little strips of yolk confetti evenly distributed over each salad. Now do the same with the whites. Garnish with the parsley and serve immediately.

> **Chef Tip:** Danish blue and Gorgonzola dolce (Italian) tend to be on the milder end of the blue cheese spectrum. Roquefort (France), Gorgonzola (Italy), Stilton (UK) and Cabrales (Spain) tend to be on the stronger and more intense end of the range. Don't you dare buy precrumbled cheese! It's never as good as the chunk or whole block.

BBQ and Ranch Southwest Chicken Salad

This is a great salad for building your knife skills. Between slicing corn off the cob, slicing onions and chopping tomatoes and romaine, you will have amazing knife skills in no time. This salad is a great application for raw sweet corn. If you prefer the corn cooked, you can boil it or microwave it until just cooked through. All good cooks need to be able to make ranch dressing. This homemade version does double duty as a dip.

Serves 4 and makes 2 cups (470 ml) ranch dressing

From-Scratch Ranch Dressing

1 cup (240 g) mayonnaise

1 cup (240 ml) buttermilk

2 tbsp (30 g) Greek yogurt

1 tsp Worcestershire sauce

¼ tsp onion powder

½ tsp kosher salt

$1/8$ tsp freshly ground black pepper

1 tbsp (3 g) finely chopped chives

1 tbsp (4 g) finely minced parsley

Salad

6 cups (280 g) chopped romaine lettuce

½ cup (80 g) diced tomato

¾ cup (120 g) fresh corn kernels

¾ cup (130 g) cooked black beans, drained

¼ cup (40 g) thinly sliced red onion

½ cup (60 g) shredded cheddar cheese

6 oz (168 g) Roast Chicken (page 38), torn into strips

Kosher salt and freshly ground pepper, to taste

½ cup (120 ml) From-Scratch Ranch Dressing (recipe above)

½ cup (120 ml) Quick and Easy Barbecue Sauce (page 53)

¼ cup (20 g) deep-fried tortilla strips

To make the dressing, add the mayonnaise, buttermilk, Greek yogurt, Worcestershire sauce and onion powder to a jar with a tight-fitting lid. Sprinkle with the salt and freshly ground black pepper. Add the chives and parsley, put the lid on and shake the jar vigorously for 30 seconds or so. Taste and adjust the seasoning. Use immediately or refrigerate for a few days.

To make the salad, divide the lettuce among 4 bowls. Arrange the tomato, corn, beans, onion and cheese in their own piles in each bowl. Place the chicken on top of each salad. Season with salt and pepper. Drizzle the ranch dressing and BBQ sauce on top. When ready to eat, toss to combine and garnish with the fried tortilla strips.

Family Gathering Italian Salad

This salad is the perfect pairing for so many dishes in this book. From spaghetti to chicken Parm and pesto pasta, this is our go-to salad for an Italian theme night. Buy a salad spinner. It's the best way to get rid of all the excess moisture in washed greens and herbs. Store washed and spun items wrapped in paper towels in zip-top bags in the fridge. They will hold for well over a week.

Serves 6–8

Classic Italian Dressing

2 cloves garlic, smashed

¾ tsp kosher salt, or to taste

¼ tsp freshly ground black pepper, or to taste

4 tbsp (60 g) mayonnaise

6 tbsp (90 ml) red wine vinegar

1 tsp dried oregano

3 tbsp (45 ml) fresh lemon juice

½ cup (120 ml) plus 2 tbsp (30 ml) extra virgin olive oil

Salad

2 cups (95 g) chopped romaine hearts

½ head radicchio, halved, cored and coarsely chopped

1 cup (70 g) coarsely chopped iceberg lettuce

2 stalks celery, thinly sliced

¼ cup (15 g) roughly chopped flat-leaf parsley

½ small red onion, thinly sliced on a mandoline

1 cup (150 g) cherry tomatoes, halved

1 cup (120 g) pitted green olives, halved

1 cup (100 g) shaved Parmigiano-Reggiano cheese

Maldon salt, to taste

To make the dressing, whisk together the dressing ingredients in a small bowl. Set aside until ready to serve. You can also double or triple this recipe and hold it in a squeeze bottle in the fridge.

To make the salad, wash all the lettuces, celery, parsley and onion under cold water. Spin dry thoroughly and wrap in paper towels to further dry as much as possible. Rinsing the onion in water removes some of its bite.

To assemble, use a very large mixing bowl and combine all the salad ingredients, reserving some cheese for garnish. Drizzle with the dressing. Toss to combine and coat all the ingredients. Taste and adjust the seasoning, then serve immediately.

Grilled Vegetable Salad with Charred Tomato Vinaigrette

This recipe is a great way to give vegetables some interest and brush up on your grilling skills. We all are trying to eat more vegetables, and this recipe makes them delicious. You know vegetables are properly grilled when they're charred but still hold their shape. If they become limp and soggy, you've grilled too far. You can dress this salad with any of your favorite dressings as well. A simple splash of balsamic and sherry vinegar is delicious.

Serves 4–6 and makes 1 cup (235 ml) dressing

Salad

1 red onion, sliced ½" (1.3 cm) thick

3 sweet bell peppers (red, orange or yellow or a mix), seeded and left in large pieces

2 small zucchini, cut in half lengthwise

Olive oil, as needed for grilling

1 tbsp (2 g) chopped fresh rosemary

Salt and freshly ground pepper, to taste

Parmesan cheese wedge, for grating

Charred Tomato Vinaigrette

8 ripe Roma or any medium-size tomatoes, halved and seeded

½ cup (120 ml) olive oil, plus more for grilling

2 cloves garlic, peeled

½ cup (12 g) torn basil leaves

2 tbsp (30 ml) champagne vinegar

Salt and freshly ground pepper, to taste

Heat a grill to high heat (500°F [260°C]).

To make the salad, toss the onion, peppers and zucchini in a large bowl with a drizzle of olive oil and season with the rosemary, salt and pepper.

To make the vinaigrette, rub the tomato halves with some olive oil. Place the tomatoes and all the vegetables on the grill and cook until well marked on each side but not too limp. The tomato skins should be lightly charred. Remove from the grill and let cool slightly.

Place the charred tomatoes, garlic and basil leaves in a food processor. Pulse until well chopped. Add the vinegar and olive oil. Purée well. Taste and season with salt and pepper as needed, and add more vinegar if the flavor is flat. Add more olive oil to smooth the consistency.

Cut the vegetables into long planks and place in a bowl. Toss with the vinaigrette and season with salt and pepper. Taste and adjust as necessary. Top with a generous grating of fresh Parmesan cheese. Serve warm or at room temperature.

> **Chef Tip:** You can grill the vegetables indoors or out. If using an outdoor grill, you can use a grill basket to keep the vegetables from falling through the grates. Don't be scared to get a good char and grill marks, which will give you more flavor.

Caesar Salad with Parmesan Frico Chips

I don't think there's salad more popular than Caesar. It seems to be the salad most people default to when they're just not sure what to eat. But that doesn't mean it should be boring or bland. When made correctly, it's easily one of the most delicious plates of food. It also requires a lot of skills from a cook's perspective. You're going to learn how to make an emulsion. You'll wash, dry and compose a salad. I'm also going to teach you how to make fricos, a fancy word for Parmesan cheese chips. I think they go great with the salad and also can be molded to give any plate some interest. For a fun twist, sprinkle the fricos with paprika or cayenne when they come out of the oven.

Serves 4

Parmesan Frico Chips
1 cup (100 g) finely shredded or grated Parmigiano-Reggiano

Caesar Salad
3 tbsp (45 ml) plus ½ cup (120 ml) extra virgin olive oil, divided

2 cloves garlic, minced

3 slices 1" (2.5-cm) thick hearty bread, cut into 1" (2.5-cm) cubes

¾ cup (75 g) grated Parmesan cheese, divided

Kosher salt and freshly ground black pepper, to taste

1 egg yolk

1 tbsp (15 ml) freshly squeezed lemon juice

2–3 anchovies

1 tsp Worcestershire sauce

2 heads romaine lettuce

Chef Tip: You can make larger frico chips and form them while they're warm. They can be formed over bowls to make a fun salad bowl. You can make cones, small and large, to serve your salad in.

To make the frico chips, preheat the oven to 375°F (190°C). Cover two large baking sheets with parchment paper.

Sprinkle 2 to 3 tablespoons (10 to 15 g) of the grated cheese to form a 4- to 4½-inch (10- to 11.3-cm) round. Spread the cheese evenly with a fork. Repeat with the rest of the mixture to get 8 fricos total, leaving 2 inches (5 cm) between each round.

Bake each sheet (one at a time) until the chips just begin to turn a pale brown and melt together, 6 to 8 minutes. Don't let them fully brown or the cheese will be bitter. While warm, use a spatula to lift the edges of the chips and loosen them from the pan. Remove the chips (keep the oven on for the croutons) and immediately lay them over a rolling pin or the side of a bottle to give them a curved shape. You can also just leave them flat as they harden. When cooled, store the chips in an airtight container for up to 2 days.

To make the salad, in a large bowl, combine 3 tablespoons (45 ml) of the olive oil with the minced garlic and whisk for 30 seconds. Add the bread cubes and toss to coat. Add ¼ cup (25 g) of the Parmesan cheese, season to taste with salt and pepper and toss again. Transfer to a baking sheet. Bake until the croutons are pale golden brown and crisp, about 15 minutes.

Combine the egg yolk, lemon juice, anchovies, Worcestershire sauce and ¼ cup (25 g) of Parmesan cheese in a small food processor. Pulse 3 to 4 times until well combined. Remove the processor top, add the remaining ½ cup (120 ml) of olive oil and process until a smooth emulsion forms. Season to taste generously with salt and pepper.

Remove the inner leaves from the romaine (save the outer leaves for another dish), wash and spin dry. Tear the large leaves into smaller pieces and leave the smaller leaves intact. Add to a large bowl, drizzle with 3 tablespoons (45 ml) of the dressing, adding more if desired, and toss to coat. Add half of the remaining ¼ cup (25 g) of cheese and three-fourths of the croutons and toss again. Transfer to a serving bowl and sprinkle with the remaining cheese and croutons. Garnish with the frico chips for crunch, and serve.

Quinoa and Arugula Grain Bowl with Tahini Dressing

The perfect salad should have a green, grain, fruit, nut and herbs, and this one truly has them all! Grain bowls are really a one-bowl wonder, and you get everything you want from them. Sometimes salads don't fill you up enough and eating too much meat in one meal can weigh you down. This grain salad will satisfy and keep you feeling fresh.

Serves 4

Dressing

¼ cup (15 g) parsley leaves

¼ cup (24 g) mint leaves

1 cup (235 ml) extra virgin olive oil

2 tbsp (30 g) tahini (sesame paste)

Zest and juice from 2 limes (about 4 tbsp [60 ml])

Zest and juice from 1 lemon (about 2 tbsp [30 ml])

2 tbsp (40 g) honey

½ tsp kosher salt, or to taste

¼ tsp ground pepper, or to taste

Salad

2 cups (370 g) cooked quinoa (follow package instructions)

2 cups (390 g) cooked brown rice (follow package instructions)

4 cups (480 g) shredded cooked chicken (from a 2½-lb [1.1-kg] rotisserie chicken)

2 Persian cucumbers, halved lengthwise and sliced on the bias

2 avocados, pitted, peeled and sliced

4 cups (135 g) watercress or baby arugula

½ cup (60 g) dried cranberries or golden raisins

½ cup (60 g) thinly sliced red onion, rinsed in cold water, blotted dry on a paper towel

½ cup (65 g) whole cashews

To make the dressing, pulse the parsley and mint in a food processor until finely chopped. Add the olive oil, tahini, citrus zest and juice, honey, salt and pepper and pulse to combine. Taste and adjust the seasoning.

To make the salad, toss the quinoa and brown rice with ½ cup (120 ml) of the dressing in a large bowl. Divide among serving bowls. Toss the chicken with ¼ cup (60 ml) of the dressing in the same large bowl. Arrange the chicken, cucumber, avocado and watercress over the quinoa-rice mixture. Top with the cranberries, red onion and cashews. Serve the remaining dressing on the side for drizzling.

Chef Tip: Feel free to substitute other dressings to keep this dish fresh and interesting. Changing out the cooked meat is also a way to customize this bowl. Carnitas (page 59) as the meat and salsa (page 72) as a dressing makes for a fun Mexican grain bowl. You're only as limited as your imagination.

Bacon and Egg Potato Salad with Greek Yogurt

Potato salad is the mother dish of all holidays and potlucks. Every cook needs to have a home-run recipe that isn't the plain yellow and white mash that looks like it came from a grocery store deli section. To get perfect creamy potatoes, always start them in cold salted water. This allows the starches to cook slowly, which will make for a creamier eating potato. Variety also matters. Red-skinned potatoes have less starch and are waxier. Dutch babies, fingerlings and Yukon gold are starchier.

Serves 6–8

1½ lb (680 g) fingerling potatoes, quartered

1¼ tsp (8 g) kosher salt, divided

8 oz (224 g) slab bacon, cut into small dice

2 tbsp (30 ml) red wine vinegar

¾ cup (180 g) Greek yogurt

3 tbsp (33 g) whole-grain mustard

6 scallions, finely chopped

1 small red onion, cut into small dice

1 tbsp (12 g) sugar

¼ tsp freshly ground pepper

2 large hard-boiled eggs, chopped

Put the potatoes in a medium-size saucepan and cover with cold water; add 1 teaspoon of the salt. Bring to a boil, then reduce the heat to medium and cook until fork tender, about 15 minutes. Meanwhile, sauté the bacon in a skillet over medium-low heat until crispy, about 12 minutes.

Drain the potatoes (do not rinse), transfer to a baking sheet and let cool for 6 to 8 minutes.

In a bowl large enough to mix the potatoes, combine the vinegar, yogurt, mustard, scallions, red onion, sugar, remaining ¼ teaspoon of salt and pepper. Transfer the potatoes to the bowl, add the bacon and hard-boiled eggs and mix by folding carefully. Serve at room temperature.

> **Chef Tip:** I've toiled for years over the perfect boiled egg method that keeps the egg nice and smooth when peeled. There are so many methods—cold start, hot start, room temperature eggs, cold eggs, it's enough to make you crazy. I've landed on cold eggs right into boiling water for 10 minutes. Shock in ice water and chill for 15 minutes.

Fresh Fruit Salad 2.0 with Honey–Citrus–Mint Dressing

Don't you dare buy cut fruit; there's no excuse for it. Buy whole fruit and cut it yourself! You'll save money because it's amazing how much fruit we prep for snacks, the kids and just to have around. Fruit salad is one of those things that we all eat often, but it needs a little overhaul. Here's the way to do it. Why wouldn't you dress a fruit salad? You dress almost every other salad, right? The dressing just helps punch up the natural flavors in the fruit. Honey kicks up the sweetness, lemon boosts the acidity and mint is just for that wow factor.

Serves 6–8

Salad

4 cups (600 g) cubed seedless watermelon

2 cups (340 g) sliced fresh strawberries

2 large fresh peaches, pitted and cut into cubes

2 large nectarines, pitted and cut into cubes

½ cup (75 g) fresh blueberries

1 cup (150 g) seedless grapes, halved

Dressing

Juice from 2 lemons (about 4 tbsp [60 ml])

1 tbsp (20 g) honey

Zest from ½ lemon

¼ cup (24 g) minced fresh mint

Mint leaves, for garnish

To make the salad, toss all the fruit together in a large bowl and reserve.

To make the dressing, whisk together the lemon juice and honey in a small bowl. Add the honey-lemon mixture, lemon zest and chopped mint to the fruit. Mix together gently. Taste and adjust the seasoning. Garnish with the mint leaves.

Chef Tip: Keep the dressing separate and dress the fruit salad right before serving, as the dressing will break down the fruit a lot faster.

Classic Chicken Stock

Stocks are the first things students learn in culinary school and are fundamental to all cooking. They are the bases of soups, sauces, rice and many more dishes. Although most home cooks use boxed or canned broths, I feel it's important to know how to make them from scratch. They're not complicated, just time-consuming, but they are worth it! A great chicken stock has deep flavor and richness from the collagen in the bones and connective tissue. For a richer stock, use necks and wings. Mirepoix is a name for the trinity of celery, carrots and onions used in making stocks and many other dishes.

Makes 12 cups (2.7 L)

4 lb (1.8 kg) chicken pieces with bones

2 stalks celery with leaves, cut into chunks

2 medium carrots, cut into chunks

2 medium onions, quartered

2 bay leaves

½ tsp dried thyme

8–10 whole peppercorns

3 qt (2.7 L) cold water

Place all the ingredients in a Dutch oven. Bring to a boil over high heat, then reduce the heat to a simmer. Simmer, uncovered, for 3 to 4 hours. Skim the foam and any debris that rises to the top every 20 minutes. Remove from the heat and allow to cool.

Set the chicken aside until cool enough to handle. Remove the meat from the bones. Discard the bones; save the meat for another use, such as chicken soup (page 108). Strain the stock, discarding the vegetables and seasonings. Refrigerate for 8 hours or overnight. Skim the fat from the surface.

Variation: Bone Broth

To make bone broth, you can double the amount of chicken bones and simmer until you have half the amount of broth than the water you started with.

Chef Tip: This is a recipe for a plain chicken stock also known as white chicken stock. You can make a brown chicken stock by simply roasting the bones in a 400°F (200°C) oven for about 45 minutes, until well browned, then follow the recipe. You can pick the meat off the bones and reserve for chicken noodle soup.

Not-Your-Grandma's Chicken Noodle Soup

Chicken noodle soup is another dish we always take for granted. We order it at restaurants or even eat it out of cans . . . bleh. A well-made chicken noodle soup from homemade chicken stock and great ingredients is transformative, almost spiritual. If you've ever had chicken soup made by a family member when you're feeling sick, you remember just how warming and restorative that meal was. That soup was an elixir, almost medicinal, and just made you feel better. I encourage you to create that experience for your family and friends. Take the time to make homemade chicken stock, pull the chicken from the bones and cut the vegetables. There are a lot of great techniques in making soup, and it won't just feed the belly but also the soul.

Serves 4

1 carrot

1 stalk celery

4 cups (960 ml) Classic Chicken Stock (page 107)

1 leek, white part only, cut into small dice

2 cups (210 g) dried rotini pasta

1 cup (140 g) cooked boneless chicken meat

Salt and freshly ground pepper, to taste

3 tbsp (12 g) finely chopped flat-leaf parsley

2 sprigs fresh thyme, leaves only

Cut the carrot in half lengthwise, then into thin half-moon pieces about ¼ inch (6 mm) thick. Cut the celery the same way as the carrot.

Bring the chicken stock to a simmer in a medium-size saucepan over medium heat. Add the carrot, celery and leek and simmer for about 15 minutes. Add the pasta and cook until al dente, 8 to 10 minutes. Add the chicken and warm through, about 1 minute. Season generously with salt to taste, then add a pinch of pepper.

Taste and adjust the seasonings. Garnish with the parsley and thyme before serving.

Warm and Comforting Butternut Squash Soup with Maple Sour Cream

It's great to know how to make puréed soups. So many of my favorite soups are puréed, including tomato, black bean and cream of anything. There are three critical steps. First, sweat the aromatics and bacon until you've extracted maximum flavor without burning. Next, boil the squash until the pieces are perfectly fork tender. Last, always purée in small batches. Never fill your blender with hot stuff higher than halfway. Many cooks have burned themselves trying to overfill hot liquid in a blender.

Serves 6–8

Soup

2 thick slices bacon

2 large cloves garlic, chopped

2 sprigs thyme

1 bay leaf

18 oz (510 g) butternut squash, peeled, seeded and cut into rough dice

4 oz (112 g) carrot, cut into rough dice

½ Granny Smith apple, peeled, cored and cut into rough dice

3 cups (705 ml) chicken stock, homemade (page 107) or low-sodium canned

1 tsp apple cider vinegar

1 tsp kosher salt

¼ tsp freshly ground black pepper

Maple Sour Cream

½ cup (120 ml) half-and-half

3 tbsp (45 g) sour cream

2 tbsp (30 ml) maple syrup

Pinch of salt

To make the soup, heat a 4- or 6-quart (3.6- or 5.4-L) Dutch oven or heavy-bottomed pot over medium heat. Lay the bacon in the pan and allow to render and brown to a crisp, 4 to 6 minutes. Remove the bacon from the pot, crumble into a bowl and reserve.

In the same pot, with the bacon drippings, add the garlic, thyme and bay leaf and cook until fragrant, about 1 minute. Add the squash pieces, carrot and apple. Stir and scrape the bottom of the pot to deglaze, about 1 minute. Add the chicken stock and scrape again to deglaze the pot. Increase the heat to medium-high and bring to a boil, then reduce to a simmer. Simmer, uncovered, for about 30 minutes.

Remove the thyme sprigs and bay leaf (the thyme leaves should be in the soup). Transfer the soup to a blender in small batches and purée. Pour into a large bowl temporarily. When all the soup is puréed, pour it back into the pot over medium heat. Add the apple cider vinegar, salt and pepper, stir thoroughly, taste and adjust the salt and pepper, if needed.

To make the maple sour cream, in a small bowl, whisk together the half-and-half, sour cream and maple syrup until smooth and even. Season with a pinch of salt. You want it to taste creamy with a touch of salty and sweet. Serve the soup with the crumbled bacon and a spoonful of maple sour cream for garnish.

> **Chef Tip:** Because this soup is puréed, it doesn't matter how straight or even the knife cuts are. So this is a great recipe to practice your slicing and dicing.

Cheesy Chicken Tortilla Soup

This is Ali's all-time favorite soup, and it's delicious! This was the first dish she cooked for date night. Tortilla soup is fortified with spices and herbs. It is also thickened with tortillas, which is a great technique to know. Techniques for soup thickening vary from roux, to rice, to this technique of using tortillas. Still other soups are thickened with bread or potato, but the tortillas give it a full mouthfeel. It's a great cooking lesson that yields a delicious dish.

Serves 4

1 cup (160 g) diced yellow or white onion

1 cup (120 g) diced carrot

1 cup (100 g) diced celery

2 tbsp (30 ml) olive oil, more if needed

2 cloves garlic, minced

1 tbsp (8 g) ancho chili powder

1 tsp dried oregano leaves

1 tsp ground cumin

¼ tsp freshly ground black pepper, or to taste

4 cups (960 ml) chicken stock, homemade (page 107) or store-bought

1 tsp kosher salt, or to taste

2 corn tortillas

1 cup (140 g) shredded roasted chicken breast (page 38)

2–3 tbsp (30–45 ml) freshly squeezed lime juice

½ cup (20 g) chopped cilantro

1 avocado, pitted, peeled and diced, for garnish

1 cup (120 g) shredded Mexican cheese blend or cheddar cheese, for garnish

3 corn tortillas, thinly sliced and deep-fried

1 lime, cut into wedges, for garnish

In a large Dutch oven over medium heat, sweat the onion, carrot and celery in the olive oil for 3 to 5 minutes, or until soft.

Add the garlic, chili powder, oregano, cumin and black pepper. Stir for 3 to 4 minutes, being careful not to burn the dry ingredients. Add more oil if needed.

Add the chicken stock and salt, bring to a boil, then reduce the heat to a low simmer and cook for about 5 minutes.

Toast the tortillas over a burner flame until slightly charred. Tear into pieces and place in a blender jar, then ladle in about 1½ cups (355 ml) of the hot soup from the pot. Carefully blend until smooth and return to the soup pot.

Add the roasted chicken to the soup and let simmer for 5 more minutes.

Just before serving, add the lime juice and cilantro. Taste and adjust the seasoning. Serve topped with lots of chopped avocado, shredded cheese, fried tortilla strips and lime wedges.

Chef Tip: If you want to add more spice, 2 to 4 sliced serrano chiles blended with the tortillas will do the trick.

Rich and Flavorful Roasted Tomato Soup

Few things are more comforting than a rich and creamy tomato soup. We like to use a great quality Italian tomato like San Marzano. This soup is as good as the brand of tomatoes you use. If using a popular commercial brand, you can boost the flavor with a little sugar and salt. Taste and adjust as you cook.

Serves 6–8

¼ cup (60 ml) olive oil

¼ cup (56 g) unsalted butter

1 medium onion, cut into small dice

1½ tsp (8 g) kosher salt

¼ cup (30 g) all-purpose flour

2 (28-oz [784-g]) cans diced tomatoes

1 cup (235 ml) chicken stock, homemade (page 107) or store-bought

1 tbsp (12 g) sugar, or to taste

¼ tsp freshly ground black pepper

⅓ cup (80 ml) half-and-half

In a medium-size, heavy-bottomed pot over medium-high heat, heat the oil and butter until melted. Add the onion and salt and sweat, stirring occasionally, until soft and translucent (no brown caramelization), 5 to 10 minutes.

Stir in the flour until the roux is slightly thickened and pale yellow, about 2 minutes. Stir in the tomatoes and their juices, chicken stock, sugar and pepper. Bring to a boil over high heat, then reduce the heat to a low simmer and cook, uncovered, for 30 minutes. Stir frequently to make sure nothing is sticking to the bottom.

Stir in the half-and-half. Remove from the heat and purée using a blender or an immersion blender. If using a blender, blend in batches and make sure you don't fill the jar more than halfway. Once the soup is smooth, return it to the heat, check for seasoning (depending on the brand of tomatoes used, additional sugar or salt may be required) and serve hot.

Chef Tips: If you want to use seasonal fresh tomatoes, for the canned tomatoes substitute 8 cups (1.4 kg) of chopped fresh tomatoes. Halve or quarter them if they are huge. Season with salt on a sheet pan and bake them at 350°F (180°C) for about 20 minutes. This will concentrate their flavor.

This could easily be completely plant based. Simply omit the half-and-half, substitute more olive oil for the butter and use vegetable stock instead of chicken stock.

After-Thanksgiving Turkey and Brown Rice Soup

I make this soup the day after Thanksgiving every year. It's a great example of creating a brown stock soup and utilizing a leftover ingredient to reduce waste. By roasting the turkey, you have browned the bones and the giblets. Using roasted bones to make stock is a classic French technique. Most people see the turkey carcass as garbage, but I see it as an opportunity to make a delicious soup. Once the turkey is carved, the festivities are over and the guests are gone, I'll immediately make the turkey stock, then I make the soup the next morning. I hope you enjoy it with your family every holiday.

Serves 12–16

1 leftover turkey carcass

4 qt (3.6 L) water

2 tbsp (28 g) unsalted butter

3 medium onions, chopped

2 large carrots, cut into medium dice

2 stalks celery, cut into medium dice

1 cup (235 ml) half-and-half

1 cup (190 g) uncooked brown rice

½ tsp dried thyme

1 tsp kosher salt

1 tsp chicken bouillon powder

Pinch of freshly ground pepper

Place the turkey carcass in a large pot that just fits and add the water. Bring the water to a boil over high heat, then reduce the heat to a simmer. Cover and simmer for about 1 hour, or until the carcass starts to fall apart. Strain the bones into a large colander and reserve the broth and carcass separately.

Let the carcass cool and pick about 3 to 4 cups (420 to 560 g) of turkey meat from the bones.

Clean the pot and return it to the stove over high heat. Melt the butter in the pot, add the onions, carrots and celery and sauté until tender, about 3 minutes. Return 4 quarts (3.6 L) of stock back to the pot. Stir in the half-and-half, rice, thyme, salt, bouillon and pepper. Reduce the heat to a simmer, cover and simmer for 30 to 35 minutes, or until the rice is tender.

Stir in the turkey meat and serve immediately.

Chef Tip: You can freeze this soup in quart-size (1-L) bags and warm them when you are craving some soup.

Classic Clam Chowda

This clam chowder recipe is a true winner—thick, creamy and very satisfying. You don't need fresh clams and juice to make great chowder. One tip for success: don't overcook your potatoes. Many chefs cook their potatoes in separate boiling water until al dente and hold in cold water. You can add the potatoes to the chowder during service time. Also, don't be shy with the salt; the potatoes and cream will absorb a lot of salt. So taste while you're cooking and taste and season again if necessary after holding in the fridge.

Serves 6–8

1½ tbsp (21 g) unsalted butter

4 slices bacon, cut into medium dice

½ onion, cut into small dice

½ cup (50 g) diced celery

2 tbsp (16 g) all-purpose flour

¼ cup (60 ml) white wine

3 large Yukon gold potatoes, cubed

2 (8-oz [235-ml]) bottles clam juice or cooking liquid from fresh clams

1 (10-oz [280-g]) can baby clams

1 cup (235 ml) chicken stock, homemade (page 107) or store-bought

3 sprigs thyme

1 bay leaf

1 cup (235 ml) heavy cream

1 cup (235 ml) half-and-half

2 tsp (12 g) kosher salt, or more to taste

Freshly ground black pepper, to taste

¼ cup (15 g) chopped fresh parsley

Oyster crackers, for serving

In a heavy Dutch oven over medium heat, add the butter and bacon and cook, stirring occasionally, until the fat has rendered and the bacon has started to brown, 5 to 7 minutes. Remove the bacon, leaving the fat in the pot, and set aside.

Add the onion and celery to the fat and cook, stirring frequently, until they are soft but not brown, about 10 minutes. Stir in the flour, making sure to work it in until the lumps are gone. Don't let the flour take on color. Add the white wine and allow the alcohol to evaporate, about 1 minute.

Stir in the potatoes, clam juice, liquid from the can of clams and chicken stock to just cover the potatoes. Add the thyme sprigs and the bay leaf. Cover the pot and simmer very gently until the potatoes are tender, 10 to 15 minutes.

When the potatoes are tender, add the cream, half-and-half, clams and reserved bacon. Season with salt and pepper to taste. Bring to a gentle simmer, NEVER letting the chowder come to a full boil. Remove the thyme and the bay leaf, and discard.

Garnish with chopped parsley and serve with oyster crackers.

> **Chef Tip:** If using fresh clams, put the clams in a large, heavy Dutch oven, add about 3 cups (705 ml) of water and set over medium-high heat. Cover and cook until the clams have opened, 10 to 15 minutes. Discard any unopened clams. Reserve the clam meat for this recipe. Strain the clam broth through a sieve lined with cheesecloth or doubled-up paper towels and use about 2 cups (480 ml).

SANDWICHES, DIPS AND SPREADS

An Intro to the Cold Kitchen (Garde Manger)

What would eating be without sandwiches and other handhelds?

We are going to break down how to create some of our favorite dishes and the components that make them. This chapter is all about bread, cheese, sauces, pickles and meat—from the best hummus and pita you've ever had to America's Vietnamese sandwich, the bánh mì. We'll also cover the ultra-trendy avocado toast.

We are all about using the best ingredients, so if you're not making bread from scratch, always source the best. We buy a few different breads and keep them frozen until ready to use. You can freeze fresh bread and pull it out a few slices at a time. Leave it out to come to room temperature, then a quick warming on a griddle or toaster oven will do the trick.

Perfect-for-Parties Baked Brie in Puff Pastry with Apricot Jam

This is a classic dish for any type of gathering, and one we always put out. Imagine a croissant filled with melted Brie cheese and sweet fruit and jam. That's what this dish is. It's a pull-apart appetizer that can be spread on toast points or eaten as is. It's one of those centerpiece starters that is the talk of the party. Puff pastry is a cook's friend. It's great for making quick pastries and even beef Wellington. We always keep a pack in the freezer.

Serves 4

1 (8-oz [224-g]) wheel of Brie
1 sheet puff pastry, frozen
3 tbsp (60 g) apricot preserves, divided
1 small Granny Smith apple, peeled and cut into small dice
¼ tsp ground cinnamon
1 egg beaten with 1 tbsp (15 ml) milk
Kosher salt and freshly ground black pepper, to taste

Preheat the oven to 400°F (200°C).

Using a large chef's knife, cut the white rind off the top of the wheel of Brie and discard. Put the disk into the freezer and at the same time pull out the sheet of puff pastry. Allow the puff pastry to thaw until it is pliable but still cold, about 30 minutes.

Roll the puff pastry to a 14 x 14–inch (35.5 x 35.5–cm) square. Using a pizza cutter or knife, cut a ½-inch (1.3-cm) wide strip from one edge of the pastry. Transfer the dough to a parchment-lined baking sheet. Place 1 tablespoon (20 g) of the preserves at the center of the pastry and then the frozen Brie wheel. Top with the apple and cinnamon, then dollop the remaining 2 tablespoons (40 g) of preserves on top. Gather the four corners of the dough, one at a time, across the Brie to enclose it completely. Tie a simple knot with the strip of dough to make a purse.

Brush the entire top and sides of the purse with the egg wash. Sprinkle with salt and pepper. If at any point the pastry seems like it's melting or too soft, put it in the freezer for 5 to 10 minutes before continuing. Make sure the pastry is well chilled before baking.

Bake on the middle rack of the oven for 30 to 40 minutes, turning the pan halfway through, until the pastry is golden brown and cooked through. Transfer to a wire rack and let cool for 8 to 10 minutes before serving warm.

> **Chef Tip:** You can swap out the preserves and fruit to whatever you like or is in season. Some great combos are blueberries with strawberry preserves, or orange marmalade and raspberries. You are only limited by your imagination.

Not-Too-Trendy Avocado Toast with Cucumber Ribbons and Pickled Red Onion

I understand why this dish is popular and loved. It has all the parts we want. The fresh toasted bread, creamy avocado, sweet-tart tomatoes, refreshing cucumber and flaky salt finish make this the perfect dish. It's easy to execute and has a high cheffy factor. We love it and make it all the time at home. Don't be scared to make it your own. Other toppings we like are togarashi (Japanese spice blend), fried egg and even some protein on top.

Serves 4

1 English cucumber

½ tsp kosher salt, plus more as needed

3 tbsp (45 ml) freshly squeezed lemon juice, divided

¼ red onion, thinly shaved on a mandoline

4 slices multigrain sourdough bread

2 ripe avocados

Maldon salt, as needed

4 tsp (20 ml) extra virgin olive oil

1 cup (150 g) cherry tomatoes, halved

1 tsp lemon zest

Cut both ends off the cucumber. Using a vegetable peeler, peel long ribbons from the cucumber, but stop when you reach the seeds. Turn the cuke over and repeat on the other side. Discard the seed portion. Place in a shallow dish, add the kosher salt and 2 tablespoons (30 ml) of the lemon juice and set aside.

In a separate bowl, combine the red onion, the remaining 1 tablespoon (15 ml) of lemon juice and a pinch of kosher salt. Set aside.

Toast the bread until deep golden brown, or to your liking. Toasting it will help the bread support the other ingredients.

Cut off the two ends of the avocados, cut the flesh in half vertically, twist the two halves, and remove the pit. This makes it easier to peel the skin from each half so it remains intact. Raising the handle of the knife, use the tip of the knife to cut each half into thin slices, keeping it orderly. Carefully push the slices over as a group so they begin to fan out. Gently tap with your palm to fan them out evenly to the width of the toast slice. Using the knife as a spatula, move it to the side and continue with the other avocado halves. Work quickly here, because avocado tends to turn brown as it is exposed to the air.

To assemble the toasts, lay out the bread slices. Pick up some cucumber ribbons, touch them lightly to a towel to remove any excess liquid and place on the toast. Again using your knife as a spatula, transfer the neatly arranged avocado slices onto the cucumber. Season with Maldon salt and drizzle 1 teaspoon of olive oil on each avocado half. Garnish each serving with cherry tomato halves and the marinated red onion. Sprinkle lemon zest before serving.

Chef Tip: Feel free to use your favorite bread in this recipe. The best slices come from a "boule" loaf. *Boule* is French for "ball," and the bread looks like a squished half ball. Slice the bread into ½- to ¾-inch (1.3- to 2-cm) slices.

From-Scratch Pita Bread

This is a nontraditional pita that produces a soft, delicious and puffy bread. Try to cook it on a pizza stone or steel if you have one. When cooked correctly, the breads will puff up and become hollow inside. Once they are cooled, you can cut them in half and use them as pita pockets. This recipe also makes for a great naan bread. For naan, roll the dough thicker (about ½ inch [1.3 cm] thick) and cook on a very hot grill on both sides.

Makes 8–10 pitas

1¼ cups (295 ml) warm water

1 tbsp (12 g) instant yeast

1½ tsp (6 g) sugar

1 extra-large egg

2 tbsp (30 ml) olive oil

¾ cup (180 g) unsweetened plain yogurt

4¾ cups (650 g) unbleached bread flour, plus more for kneading

½ tsp baking powder

1½ tsp (9 g) salt

Classic Hummus (page 124), for serving

In the mixing bowl of a stand mixer, combine the warm water, instant yeast and sugar. Stir with a whisk until it's combined. Let it stand until a thick raft forms on top, 10 to 15 minutes.

In a separate bowl, beat the egg, olive oil and yogurt until well combined. Add this to the water-yeast mixture.

Add the bread flour, baking powder and salt to the mixture and knead on low speed with the dough hook attachment for 10 minutes. Stop the mixer and scrape down the sides of the bowl, releasing the dough from the sides. Continue mixing on low speed until the dough completely pulls away from the sides of the bowl, about 5 more minutes. The dough should be smooth, soft and slightly sticky.

Remove the bowl from the mixer and scrape down the sides of the bowl, releasing the dough. Cover with a towel or plastic wrap and let stand in a warm spot in the kitchen until it doubles in volume, about 1 hour.

Turn out the dough onto a very lightly floured work surface. Gently deflate the dough by punching it down. Measure it into 2- to 3-ounce (56- to 84-g) portions. Round the portions into balls and space them 2 inches (5 cm) apart on a sheet pan lightly dusted with flour. Cover loosely with a towel or plastic wrap. Let stand in a warm spot for 15 to 20 minutes, or until the balls are puffy and tender when poked with a finger.

Roll the balls into 6- to 8-inch (15- to 20-cm) rounds ¼ inch (6 mm) thick. Lightly dust them with flour to prevent the rounds from sticking to each other.

Place a pizza stone or steel in the oven and preheat to its highest temperature for at least 30 minutes. Carefully slide the dough rounds onto the pizza stone and bake for 1 to 2 minutes. Once the rounds brown and puff and fill with air, remove from the oven. Stack them on top of each other to prevent the rounds from drying out. Serve with hummus for dipping.

> **Chef Tip:** You can freeze the dough balls before proofing for months in zip-top bags. When ready to bake, transfer from the freezer to the fridge for 24 hours, where they will thaw and proof. Let them stand in a warm place for about 30 minutes before rolling and baking.

Classic Hummus

Hummus has become so ubiquitous that we take it for granted. Most people don't think twice and buy it from the store. But homemade hummus is much more delicious than store-bought and very easy to make! We think the stuff from the supermarket has a sour flavor that comes from additives that don't need to be there. Our recipe is super creamy and smooth and has great flavor.

Makes 2 ½ cups (590 g)

1 (15-oz [420-g]) can chickpeas, with their liquid

2 tbsp (30 ml) fresh lemon juice

2 cloves garlic, roughly chopped

⅓ cup (80 g) sesame tahini (stir from bottom before measuring)

1½ tsp (9 g) kosher salt

¼ tsp ground cumin

¾ cup (180 ml) extra virgin olive oil, plus more for drizzling

Paprika, for garnish

In a food processor, combine the chickpeas with the liquid from the can, lemon juice, garlic, tahini, salt and cumin. Process until combined. With the processor running, add the olive oil a little at a time, until the hummus is smooth but still thick. Occasionally scrape down the sides of the processor so everything is evenly combined.

Taste and don't be afraid to add more salt, lemon juice and/or cumin to your preference.

Smooth the hummus in a shallow dish. Garnish with extra virgin olive oil and sprinkle with paprika.

> **Chef Tip**: The secret to creamy hummus is a high percentage of tahini, which is very fine sesame seed paste. The other secret is aquafaba, the liquid from boiling down the chickpeas. This magic potion has emulsifying properties similar to egg whites. Whipping the aquafaba into the hummus makes it extra creamy.

My Favorite Tuna Sandwich

You've been fooled into thinking butter is the best fat for toasting bread. But chefs have been using the real secret fat for years: mayonnaise! It's been sitting there in your fridge underutilized your whole life. Mayonnaise is made by emulsifying oil and eggs, then seasoning with some tang and spices. No wonder it's the best for toasting because it crisps, brings richness and seasons all at the same time. Use this secret to make my tuna sandwich, but it's also perfect for grilled cheese and anywhere you need to toast bread.

Makes 4 sandwiches

Tuna Salad

2 (5-oz [142-g]) cans solid white tuna in water, drained well

¼ cup (60 g) mayonnaise

¼ cup (60 g) Greek yogurt

¼ cup (30 g) finely diced celery

3 tbsp (30 g) finely diced red onion

1½ tsp (4 g) lemon pepper, or to taste

Sandwiches

5 tbsp (75 g) mayonnaise

8 slices Texas toast bread

4 slices cheddar or American cheese

4 tsp (16 g) yellow mustard

8 leaves Bibb or butter lettuce

8 thin slices tomato

Kosher salt, to taste

To make the tuna salad, put the tuna into a sieve and press well to remove the liquid. In a medium-size bowl, combine the tuna, mayonnaise, yogurt, celery and onion. Smash with the back of a fork until the tuna is loose and the mixture is well combined. Season with the lemon pepper.

To make the sandwiches, smear 1 teaspoon of the mayonnaise on each side of each piece of bread. Toast one side of each slice of bread in a dry pan over medium heat for 2 to 3 minutes, until golden brown and crisp. Flip the slices over and add a slice of cheese to 4 pieces of bread while it is still hot. Toast on that side with the cheese on top. Once the bottom is golden, 1 to 2 minutes, remove from the heat.

Smear 1 teaspoon of the mustard on the bottom slice of bread (without the cheese) and add 3 ounces (84 g) of tuna salad. Top with the lettuce and tomato slices. Season the tomato with kosher salt, and add the top slice of bread.

> **Chef Tip:** Make the ultimate tuna melt by using two slices of sharp cheddar cheese per sandwich. Melt one slice onto each piece of Texas toast, then stuff with the tuna salad. You can thank me later.

Pork Bánh Mì with Pickled Vegetables and Pâté

Here is another dish from my first book that I believe all cooks should know. Bánh mì are the hottest sandwiches in the United States, and you don't have to find a Vietnamese bánh mì shop to enjoy one. The trick here is to make the roasted shaved pork at home. The secret is brining the pork before roasting. Try to find very light, airy baguettes or French rolls. A good bánh mì should be crispy on the outside and light and airy in the middle.

Serves 2–3

Roast Pork
10 cups (2.4 L) cold water, divided
½ cup (144 g) kosher salt
½ cup (100 g) sugar
3 medium cloves garlic, peeled
1 medium serrano chile, crushed
1 tbsp (8 g) cracked black peppercorns
1½ lb (680 g) boneless pork shoulder

Pickled Carrot
½ cup (120 ml) distilled white vinegar
½ cup (100 g) sugar
1 tsp kosher salt
1½ cups (180 g) matchstick-cut carrot

Bánh Mì
6–8" (15–20-cm) center piece of French baguette (not sourdough)
4 tbsp (60 g) mayonnaise, divided
3 oz (84 g) pork pâté, divided (optional)
1 large English cucumber, shaved into ribbons with a peeler
¼ cup (10 g) cilantro leaves
1 jalapeño, very thinly sliced
2 tsp (10 ml) light soy sauce

To make the pork, bring 2 cups (470 ml) of the water to a simmer in a small saucepan. Stir in the salt and sugar and keep stirring or whisking until all the solids have completely dissolved. Turn off the heat and add the garlic, chile and peppercorns. The heat will make all their flavors open up. Pour the warm brine into a 6-quart (5.4-L) container large enough to hold the pork and 10 cups (2.4 L) of liquid. Pour in the remaining 8 cups (1.9 L) of cold water. Add the pork, cover and refrigerate overnight.

Preheat the oven to 400°F (200°C) and arrange a rack in the middle.

Remove the pork from the brine, use a ton of paper towels to pat it very dry and place it fat-side up in a roasting pan. Allow it to come to room temperature for about 30 minutes. Roast the pork until the internal temperature reaches 165°F (74°C), about 1 hour and 45 minutes. Let it cool to room temperature, at least 45 minutes, then slice thinly, about ⅛ inch (3 mm) thick.

To make the pickled carrot, combine the vinegar, sugar and salt in a small saucepan over medium heat. Stir constantly, and once the sugar and salt have dissolved, remove the saucepan from the heat. Add the carrot and stir to coat in the pickling mixture. Let stand until the carrot has softened, at least 30 minutes or up to overnight. Drain well and set aside. You can make this days ahead and keep refrigerated in an airtight container.

To assemble the bánh mì, slice off the top one-third of the baguette lengthwise and set aside. Remove enough of the bottom interior of the bread so that the filling can fit easily. Spread 2 tablespoons (30 g) of the mayonnaise on the top part and 2 tablespoons (30 g) on the bottom. Spread half of the pâté, if using, on the bottom section and half on the top section. Top it with the sliced pork (there may be some sliced pork left over, so smash it into your mouth and enjoy while building the bánh mì). Then add the cucumber, cilantro leaves, pickled carrot and jalapeño. Sprinkle with the soy sauce and close with the upper half of the baguettes.

> **Chef Tip:** Combine the pâté and mayonnaise in a food processor to make a spread. You can also used cold cuts here for the roast pork to save a step. You can also swap out half the carrots for daikon radish for some extra deliciousness.

Spinach and Three-Cheese Quesadilla

Quesadillas, like pizza, are the perfect food—cheese, bread and veggies all in one hot, melted package. This recipe is written with flour tortillas, but you can use any large tortilla you love. We use corn and flavored tortillas all the time. Quesadillas are also a cheffy tool. Add some steak or roasted chicken and your favorite veggies or greens to make it extra special.

Makes 4 quesadillas

2 oz (56 g) grated Parmesan cheese

2 oz (56 g) grated mozzarella cheese

2 oz (56 g) grated cheddar cheese

1 (10-oz [280-g]) package frozen spinach, thawed and drained well

4 (8" [20-cm]) flour tortillas

¼ cup (40 g) minced yellow onion

Kosher salt and freshly ground black pepper, to taste

Pan spray, as needed

Blend the cheeses together with your fingers in a small bowl and set aside. Place the drained spinach on a paper towel to remove excess moisture. Place a large nonstick pan or skillet over medium heat.

Place the tortillas on a clean work surface. Working on only the lower halves, add 1½ ounces (42 g) of cheese, 1 ounce (28 g) of spinach and 1 tablespoon (10 g) of onion to each tortilla. Then top with the remaining cheese mixture to cover. The cheeses are usually salty enough, but season with salt and pepper if desired. Fold the tortillas in half to make half-moons.

Spray the preheated skillet with pan spray for about 3 seconds to coat. Place the filled tortillas in batches in the skillet and cook for about 3 minutes, until you see the cheese starting to melt and the tortilla is light brown. Turn the quesadilla over and continue to cook for another 3 minutes, until the cheese is fully melted. Remove from the heat and serve immediately. Or you can hold the cooked quesadillas on a sheet pan, then warm them in a 350°F (180°C) oven until the cheese is warm and gooey.

Chef Tip: You can get creative with the cheeses. We love smoked Gouda, Brie and even blue cheeses for quesadillas. A dollop of your favorite preserves makes them epic.

Great-for-a-Gathering Steak Sandwich with Sriracha Mayonnaise

All great cooks need that showstopper sandwich, the one that looks like it will take ten people to devour, the sandwich that makes everyone stop dead in their tracks and beg for a piece. This is that sandwich. Using a large loaf of flat country bread like focaccia is key. Slice it in half through the center to make one giant sandwich.

Serves 4-6

Steak

1½ tsp (9 g) kosher salt, plus more as needed

¼ tsp freshly ground black pepper, plus more as needed

6 tbsp (90 ml) olive oil

6 medium cloves garlic, minced or pressed through a garlic press (about 2 tbsp [20 g])

1 medium shallot, minced (about 3 tbsp [30 g])

2 tbsp (4 g) minced fresh rosemary

2 lb (910 g) skirt steak, trimmed but not butterflied, if possible (or use flap meat or flank steak)

Sriracha Aioli

1 cup (240 g) mayonnaise

2 cloves garlic, minced, or to taste

1 tbsp (15 ml) freshly squeezed lemon juice

2 tbsp (30 ml) Sriracha sauce, or to taste

Sandwiches

2 loaves flat rustic bread, such as ciabatta or focaccia

Olive oil, for brushing

2 medium tomatoes, thinly sliced

Salt and freshly ground pepper, to taste

8 oz (224 g) cheddar cheese, sliced or shredded

1½ cups (30 g) arugula

To make the steak, pulse the salt, pepper, olive oil, garlic, shallot and rosemary in a blender until a rough paste forms, scraping down the blender jar as needed. Thoroughly coat each piece of meat in the marinade and reserve in a gallon-size (3.6-L) zip-top bag; press out as much air as possible and seal the bag. Refrigerate for 1 hour, flipping the bag after 30 minutes to ensure that the meat marinates evenly.

To make the aioli, in a small bowl, combine all the aioli ingredients. Cover and chill well until needed.

Preheat your grill to its highest setting for at least 5 to 10 minutes. Remove the steak from the marinade and pat dry with paper towels. Season lightly again with salt and pepper. Grill, uncovered, using a small sauté pan as a weight, until well marked on the first side, about 4 minutes, depending on thickness. Using tongs, flip the steak and grill until the thickest part of the meat is slightly less done than desired, 3 to 4 minutes for medium-rare (about 130°F [54°C]) or 6 to 8 minutes for medium (about 135°F [57°C]). If the exterior of the meat is browned but the steak is not yet cooked through, move the steak to a cooler side of the grill and continue to cook to your desired doneness. Season with salt and pepper, if needed.

Transfer the steaks to a cutting board; tent loosely with foil and let rest for 5 minutes. Slice the steak very thinly on the bias.

To make the sandwiches, split each loaf horizontally, brush a bit of oil on the inside and grill for about 1 minute, until warm and slightly toasted. Season the tomato slices with salt and pepper, if desired.

Spread some aioli on both halves of the bread. Layer the steak on the bottom. Place the cheese on the steak, then the arugula and then the tomato. Add the top of the loaf, slice the entire sandwich in half and enjoy!

> **Chef Tip:** You have a lot of options when it comes to the steak for this sandwich. Look for flap meat, carne asada or even prime rib. You could roast a prime rib (page 28) and shave it thinly for the ultimate steak sandwich.

VEGETABLES

Learn the Best Cooking Methods to Get Maximum Flavor and Perfect Texture

As a culture, we've forgotten how to cook vegetables well. They have become an afterthought, those things you're supposed to finish in order to get your dessert. We've canned them, frozen them and cooked all life out of them. Only in the last few decades have we started to appreciate them again and largely thanks to the farmers' markets. Thanks to seasonal fruit, now we are remembering that seasonal vegetables picked ripe and cooked thoughtfully are absolutely delicious.

We like to approach cooking vegetables like cooking meat: with respect and care. We use multiple styles of cooking and both moist and dry heat. We use assertive seasonings, like vinaigrettes, agrodolces and crème fraîche. We're not messing around here, because a perfectly cooked vegetable is just as delicious as any steak or roast.

So how do we do this, you ask? Remember your fundamentals. Unlike meat, veggies don't contain any or much fat or protein. And it's the fat and protein that are loaded with savoriness. Veggies do have a lot of sugar, though, but you have to unlock it with browning, charring or roasting.

It's all about accentuating what vegetables already have, which is a deep, earthy sweetness and in some cases bitterness. As a cook, you need to add the savoriness, acidity and fat in the forms of sauces, marinades and aggressive cooking techniques.

Vegetables also usually contain a lot of moisture, so cook them quickly with very high heat. Slow cooking will cause them to get soggy and lose all the delicious properties we want to exploit.

Roasted Cauliflower Steak with Agrodolce, Golden Raisins and Pine Nuts

Agrodolce is the Italian version of a sweet and sour sauce. It's a great sauce to know and serve with vegetables like cauliflower in this dish, as well as fish and meats, especially game meats. It is slightly sticky and made from vinegar and sugar. We love adding raisins and a touch of heat in the form of red pepper flakes. This dish is a must-cook vegetarian main course. Even though we're not vegetarians, we eat this dish all the time.

Serves 4

2 heads cauliflower, cut vertically into ¾'' (2-cm) thick steaks (4 to 6 steaks total)

Extra virgin olive oil, for drizzling

Kosher salt and freshly ground black pepper, to taste

1½ cups (355 ml) red wine vinegar

¼ cup (60 ml) balsamic vinegar

⅓ cup (50 g) golden raisins

½ tsp crushed red pepper flakes, or to taste

2 tbsp (18 g) pine nuts, lightly toasted

Maldon salt, for garnish

Preheat the oven to 475°F (240°C).

Place the cauliflower steaks on a baking sheet. Drizzle with olive oil and sprinkle with kosher salt and pepper on both sides. Transfer to the oven and bake until golden brown but still al dente, 18 to 20 minutes.

Meanwhile, in a small saucepan, bring the red wine vinegar, balsamic vinegar, golden raisins and red pepper flakes to a boil over high heat, and then lower the heat to a simmer. Let simmer and reduce for 5 to 7 minutes, until syrupy.

Transfer the roasted cauliflower to a serving platter. Pour the raisin sauce over the top. Sprinkle with the pine nuts and a bit of Maldon salt.

> **Chef Tip:** Browning (aka caramelization) is critical to this recipe. If you're not seeing the brown on the cauliflower, keep it in the oven until you do. The flavor really is in the browning. If you feel comfortable starting the "steaks" in a preheated cast-iron pan, then transferring to the oven, that will give the ultimate browning.

Fresh Sweet Corn Pudding

This delicious dish eats like a sweet corn soufflé. It's fluffy, decadent and deceptively light. We love it as a side dish for the holidays or with a big meat centerpiece. The sweetness of the corn pairs well with a rich main dish, such as roast chicken (page 38), prime rib (page 28) or braised short ribs (page 25). It's a must for sweet corn season. As easy to cook as it is to eat, this dish will give you instant chef cred at a potluck.

Serves 8-10

Softened butter, for greasing
⅓ cup (68 g) sugar
3 tbsp (24 g) all-purpose flour
2 tsp (6 g) baking soda
½ tsp salt
7 large eggs
2 cups (470 ml) whipping cream
½ cup (120 ml) melted butter
6 cups (960 g) fresh corn kernels (from about 8 ears)

Preheat the oven to 350°F (180°C). Generously butter an 11 x 7–inch (28 x 17.5–cm) baking dish and set aside.

In a medium-size bowl, whisk together the sugar, flour, baking soda and salt until combined. In another medium-size bowl, whisk together the eggs, cream and melted butter until smooth and even, about 2 minutes.

Gradually whisk the dry mixture into the wet. Whisk until just combined and smooth. Fold in the corn just until evenly distributed. Don't overdo it here or you'll make this pudding too dense.

Pour the corn batter into the baking dish and bake for 45 to 60 minutes, until the top is golden brown and delicious and the center is just set. You can check it by inserting a cake tester; it should come out dry and clean.

Remove the pudding from the oven and let rest for at least 5 minutes before serving.

> **Chef Tips:** You can substitute fresh corn with frozen. If you are feeling a little guilty about calories, you can substitute half the cream with milk. I also double this recipe and cook it in a large Dutch oven for gatherings of 12 or more.

Steak House Creamed Spinach with Bacon

Creamed spinach will forever be a steak house classic. It's also a fundamental technique. If you can cook creamed spinach, you can make creamed corn, creamed leeks and cream sauce. Roux is the fundamental thickening technique, where the fat turns the flour into a sponge that slowly absorbs liquid. The flour bonds with the liquid to make a sauce. You can make that sauce as thick or as thin as you desire. That's all creamed spinach or corn is—vegetables suspended in a thick, seasoned roux. I add bacon to my version for a smoky, savory note.

Serves 4–6

2 (10-oz [280-g]) packages frozen chopped spinach, thawed

4 slices bacon

½ yellow onion, minced

2 cloves garlic, minced

2 tbsp (16 g) all-purpose flour

1 tsp seasoned salt

½ tsp freshly ground black pepper

1½ cups (355 ml) milk

½ cup (120 ml) heavy cream

Drain the spinach well and squeeze out the excess moisture with your hands; chop finely and set aside.

Cook the bacon in a heavy skillet over medium heat until crisp, 6 to 8 minutes; remove, drain and crumble. Remove all but 2 tablespoons (30 ml) of the bacon drippings. Sauté the onion and garlic in the bacon grease until just starting to turn golden, 2 to 4 minutes. Add the flour, seasoned salt and pepper and stir to combine; cook for about 1 minute.

Slowly add the milk, stirring constantly until the flour and milk are incorporated and slightly thick. Stir in the spinach and bacon until incorporated and heated through, about 3 minutes. Add the cream, taste and adjust the seasoning if necessary.

Chef Tip: You can always play with portions of cream to milk in these recipes. If you're trying to cut down on calories, take the total amount of dairy and substitute it with milk or even skim milk. It won't have the same creaminess, but you'll save on fat.

Crispy Cast-Iron Roasted Brussels Sprouts with Bacon

Brussels sprouts get a bad rap but are some of the tastiest vegetables ever. The secret is they need to be caramelized by dry heat like roasting or frying to unlock their sweetness and texture. People boiling Brussels sprouts ruined the vegetable for so many. Let's change all that. Remember these three tips. First, be sure to brown the sprouts and get some crispy leaves. Second, season generously. And third, keep them al dente inside, so they'll have some texture.

Serves 4

1 lb (454 g) Brussels sprouts

4 tbsp (60 ml) extra virgin olive oil or bacon drippings

3–4 cloves garlic, smashed

½ tsp kosher or Maldon salt

¼ tsp freshly ground black pepper

2 thyme sprigs

2 slices thick-cut bacon, cooked and cut into bite-size pieces

2 tbsp (30 ml) balsamic vinegar

1 tbsp (15 ml) freshly squeezed lemon juice

Preheat the oven to 400°F (200°C).

Trim the bottom of each Brussels sprout, then slice each in half from top to bottom. Heat the olive oil (or bacon drippings, if using) in a cast-iron pan over medium-high heat until it shimmers. Put the sprouts cut-side down in one layer in the pan. Add the garlic, sprinkle with the salt and pepper and add the thyme sprigs.

Cook, undisturbed, until the sprouts begin to turn golden brown on the bottom, 4 to 6 minutes.

Add the cooked bacon pieces and transfer the pan to the oven. Continue to roast, shaking the pan every 5 minutes, until the sprouts are quite brown and tender, 15 to 18 minutes. Pierce the stemmy core of a few sprouts with the tip of a paring knife to check for tenderness.

Add the balsamic vinegar and lemon juice, and stir to coat. Remove the thyme sprigs. Taste and adjust with more salt and pepper if necessary. Serve hot or warm.

> **Chef Tip:** Cast iron is the best pan for deep browning on the stove and finishing in the oven because of its heavy build and ability to hold heat.

Flash-Grilled Asparagus with Lemon Zest

The secret to perfectly cooked asparagus is very high dry heat. They contain a lot of moisture, so moderate heat steams them limp and lifeless. They cook like shrimp or scallops and need an aggressive sear to get the exteriors browned while leaving the interiors crispy. They come in different thickness, but most are thin. The thicker the asparagus, the lower the heat. Super thick green and white asparagus should be boiled slightly and then just finished on the grill. Thin asparagus should never be boiled, just roasted or grilled over very high heat.

Serves 4

1 lemon

1 lb (454 g) medium asparagus, snapped and/or trimmed

½ tsp kosher salt

¼ tsp freshly ground black pepper

2 cloves garlic, smashed and minced

3 tbsp (45 ml) olive oil

Pan spray

Run the lemon on a microplane grater to remove the yellow zest only, not the white pith. Now cut the lemon in half and reserve it for grilling.

Place the asparagus in a large bowl, season with the salt, pepper and garlic and drizzle with the olive oil. Give the asparagus a good massage between your fingers to coat it well with the seasonings.

Preheat a grill pan over high heat for 5 to 7 minutes, or until it gets screaming hot (600°F [315°C]). Fold a large paper towel in half, then in half again and then in half one last time. Spray the towel with 3 to 5 seconds of pan spray and, using tongs, run it on the grill pan ridges.

Place the lemon halves on the grill, cut-side down, and sear. Lay the asparagus perpendicular to the grill ridges. Once good grill marks are evident, turn to other sides, until well charred and tender, 5 to 8 minutes total. Your lemon halves will be well charred by then. Remove from the heat and allow to cool. Plate the asparagus, sprinkle with the lemon zest, squeeze the charred lemon halves over (through a small sieve to catch the seeds) and serve immediately.

> **Chef Tips:** Asparagus bottoms are very tough, woody and not pleasant to eat. To find out how much of the bottom to cut off, take one asparagus and hold it at the bottom and in the middle. Flex until it snaps. Now you know where the bottoms will be tough and woody. Cut the rest of the bunch at that snap point.
>
> There's no need to peel medium asparagus unless you hate the waxy feel and slippery taste. But you MUST peel any asparagus thicker than your thumb because the peel will be stringy.

Elote: Mexican Street Corn with Cotija Cheese and Crema

Mexican street corn can be found at street vendors in so many cities. Now chefs have adapted it and elevated an already delicious dish. My version uses pumpkin seeds for crunch and ancho chile for a smoky, spicy note. This corn on the cob will steal the show at any meal with the fancy husk tied back. The most underrated piece of kitchen equipment is the microwave. I've used the code "Chef Mike" for the microwave in some of the restaurants I've worked at over the years. Chef Mike is great for warming, steaming and bringing cold rice back from rigid chalky crystals to soft and pillowy. Chef Mike is also perfect for parcooking the corn in this recipe.

Makes 6 ears

½ cup (65 g) pumpkin seeds

Maldon salt, to taste

6 ears fresh corn, husks on

¾ cup (180 g) mayonnaise

3 limes, divided

1 tsp ancho chile powder, plus more as needed

Freshly ground black pepper, to taste

1 cup (120 g) crumbled cotija cheese (or substitute Pecorino Romano or Parmesan)

¼ cup (10 g) chopped fresh cilantro

Preheat the oven to 325°F (170°C).

Spread the pumpkin seeds (pepitas) on a small sheet pan and toast for 2 to 5 minutes. Coarsely chop and season with salt. Set aside.

Peel back the outer husk of the corn, but leave it attached. Remove the silk, then replace the husk, covering the kernels.

Arrange the corn in a microwave-safe dish and cover with a moist paper towel. Cook for 7 to 9 minutes, depending on how strong Mike is.

Meanwhile, in a small bowl, mix together the mayonnaise, zest and juice of 2 limes, chile powder, and salt and pepper to taste.

Pull back the husks and tie using a strip of the husk, if desired (this makes a nice presentation). Slather the hot corn with the mayonnaise mixture and sprinkle with the cheese, cilantro and pepitas. Cut the remaining lime into wedges and serve alongside the corn.

> **Chef Tip:** You can use any method to cook the corn. For moist heat, you can boil or steam. For dry heat, grilling or roasting in the oven works great.

Not-Your-Grandmother's Sautéed Green Beans with Slivered Almonds

BSD is a chef acronym you should know. It stands for blanch, shock and drain, and it applies to many vegetables that need precooking at restaurants. Blanching helps take the raw bite out of vegetables but keeps their texture. Once blanched, shocking in ice water stops the cooking process. Then draining removes any excess moisture and gets them ready for seasoning or sauce. This is a great technique for parcooking and holding all vegetables. It cooks the vegetable about 90 percent. Then all you need to do is finish cooking and season as you wish!

Serves 4

Kosher salt, for blanching water

1 lb (454 g) green beans, trimmed

3 tbsp (42 g) unsalted butter

3 oz (84 g) slivered almonds

2 medium cloves garlic, thinly sliced

1 medium shallot, thinly sliced

1½ tbsp (23 ml) freshly squeezed lemon juice

1 tsp Maldon salt, or to taste

½ tsp freshly ground black pepper, or to taste

Zest from 1 lemon

Bring a large pot of salted water to a boil and prepare an ice bath. For the ice bath, use a lot of ice, add 1 teaspoon or so of salt (which will make it a bit colder) and put a colander inside the bowl so that the ice stays separate from the beans and it's easy to drain the beans as soon as they are well chilled.

Add the green beans to the boiling water and cook until tender-crisp, about 3 minutes. Ladle out 2 tablespoons (30 ml) of the water, then transfer the green beans to the ice bath using a wire mesh spider or tongs. Allow to chill completely, then lift the colander out of the ice bath, and dry the green beans thoroughly with kitchen towels or paper towels. This can be done ahead of time.

In a medium-size skillet, heat the butter and almonds over medium heat and cook, stirring frequently, until the almonds are deeply browned and nutty, 2 to 4 minutes. Add the garlic and shallot and cook, stirring often, until lightly browned, about 2 minutes longer. Add the lemon juice, along with 1 to 2 tablespoons (15 to 30 ml) of the cooking water. Increase the heat to high and stir and shake the pan rapidly to emulsify, about 30 seconds. The sauce should have a glossy sheen and not appear watery or greasy. If it's still watery, continue to simmer and shake. If it looks greasy, add another 1 tablespoon (15 ml) of water. When the sauce is ready, remove from the heat.

Add the green beans to the pan with the sauce and toss to coat and combine. Return to medium heat and cook, tossing, until heated through, about 1 minute. Season to taste with Maldon salt and fresh black pepper. Garnish with the lemon zest and serve immediately.

> **Chef Tip:** We like Blue Lake green beans because they are larger then the French haricots verts. They hold their texture and do well after the BSD. Haricots verts tend to get soggy because they are so thin and delicate.

Smashed Crispy Potatoes with Chives and Sour Cream

These potatoes are a fancy side dish or starter. It's like a potato chip crossed with a twice-baked potato—yum! You can get very creative with these. For tailgates, add some bacon and cheddar cheese before baking. To get a little fine dining flavor, add some crème fraîche and caviar! These are a great culinary base for deliciousness.

Serves 4

1½ lb (680 g) baby gold or yellow potatoes

1 tbsp (18 g) kosher salt

3 tbsp (42 g) unsalted butter

2 tbsp (30 ml) olive oil

Maldon salt and freshly ground pepper, to taste

1 cup (240 g) sour cream

¼ cup (12 g) chopped fresh chives

Place the potatoes in a large saucepan; add cold water to cover by 1 inch (2.5 cm) and add the kosher salt. Bring to a boil over high heat, then reduce the heat to medium and simmer until the potatoes are soft when pierced with a paring knife, 20 to 25 minutes. Drain well in a colander and reserve.

Preheat the oven to 350°F (180°C).

Place the potatoes on a parchment-lined half sheet pan. Use a large fork or potato masher to smash each potato flat but still keep them in one piece; they should be ¼ to ½ inch (0.6 to 1.3 cm) thick. Surface area equals crispy and crunchy.

Melt the butter and olive oil together in the microwave in a small bowl. Drizzle each potato with the butter/olive blend, then sprinkle with Maldon salt and pepper.

Transfer to the oven and bake for 30 to 40 minutes, or until deep golden and crispy. While the potatoes are baking, stir together the sour cream, chives and a pinch of salt. Remove the potatoes from the oven and serve warm, topping each with a dollop of the sour cream.

Chef Tips: If you are making a lot of these for a meal or an event, you can use a steamer. Also, to mash a lot at once, place cooked and drained potatoes on a parchment-lined half sheet pan. Spray the tops generously with pan spray, lay another piece of parchment on top and then smash with another pan on top of that.

Super Fluffy and Buttery Mashed Potatoes

Every cook must know how to make mashed potatoes. There are some critical steps: Start with a starchy potato like Yukon gold or russet, not a waxy potato like red skin. Leave the potato pieces large, at least 2 inches (5 cm), so they don't get waterlogged and become mealy. Start in cold water so the starches cook slowly and become creamy. The finer the mash, the fluffier the texture. We love mashers and ricers with small holes to get the potatoes super fine. This will guarantee amazing mashed potatoes.

Serves 4

6 tbsp (84 g) unsalted butter

2 lb (910 g) Yukon gold potatoes, peeled and cut into 2" (5-cm) pieces

1–2 tbsp (18–36 g) kosher salt

½ cup (120 ml) half-and-half

Cut the butter into 3 pieces and let soften slightly.

Place the peeled potato chunks into a large saucepan; add cold water to cover by 1 inch (2.5 cm) and add 1 tablespoon (18 g) of the salt. Bring to a boil over high heat, then reduce the heat to medium and simmer until the potatoes break apart when a paring knife is inserted, 15 to 18 minutes. Drain the potatoes well, return to the saucepan and place back on the burner over low heat.

Warm the half-and-half in a microwave-safe container for about 45 seconds, until steaming. Using a potato masher, mash the potatoes until a few small lumps remain. Add the warm half-and-half to the potatoes; using a rubber spatula, fold well. Then add one piece of butter at a time, folding it in gently to emulsify the butter into the potatoes. Season with a two-finger pinch of salt, or to taste. Serve immediately.

> **Chef Tip:** Roasted garlic, chives and wasabi are all fun add-ins to give your mashed potatoes some variety.

Double-Fried French Fries with Garlic Aioli

Most people take French fries for granted. A well-made French fry is perfection: crispy on the outside and fluffy and starchy inside, salty and, in our case, garlicky with herbs. I think we've eaten thousands of subpar, frozen fries drenched in ketchup, and even so-so fries are still delicious. The technique of double frying is a great one and should be utilized for a multitude of dishes and ingredients. Apply this to fried chicken, potato chips and any dish that needs to be cooked through and then crisped up to finish.

Serves 4–6

Garlic Aioli
2–3 peeled garlic cloves minced

Salt and pepper, to taste, divided

2 egg yolks, separated

1 cup (240 ml) extra virgin olive oil, divided

1 tablespoon (15 ml) fresh lemon juice

4 medium cloves garlic, finely minced

About ¼ cup (10 g) total of chopped fresh herbs (such as parsley, sage, rosemary and thyme)

2 tbsp (6 g) minced chives

3 large russet or Kennebec potatoes (about 2½ lb [1.1 kg])

Pan spray

Vegetable oil, for deep-frying

Kosher salt, to taste

Chef Tips: You can freeze the fries after the initial fry once they've cooled. Once frozen, transfer them to zip-top bags for storage. You can drop them right into a hot fryer from a frozen state.

To contain the bubbling oil, don't fill a fryer pot more than half the height of the pot. Keep the lid nearby to cover the pot in case of emergency. Never try to extinguish a grease fire with water.

To make the aioli, place the garlic in a blender with a large pinch of kosher salt and ground pepper. Pulse 3 to 4 times to finely mince the garlic.

Add the egg yolks and run the blender for about 2 to 3 seconds until the yolks are whipped and creamy yellow in color. With the blender running on low, slowly pour in half of the olive oil in a tiny stream. Add the lemon juice. Gradually stream in the remaining olive oil and process until the mixture thickens and emulsifies. Transfer to a small bowl; add salt, pepper, and any other seasonings of choice. Cover and chill well.

Fill a medium-size bowl with cool tap water. In a large bowl, combine the garlic, herbs and chives.

Wash the potato skins well. We like to leave the peel on, but you don't have to. Coat a knife with a bit of pan spray to keep it from sticking to the potato. Cut a ⅜-inch (1-cm) slice off one side of the potato. Place the potato on this flat side and cut the rest of the potato into ¼-inch (6-mm) tiles. Stack the tiles and cut into ¼-inch (6-mm) lengths. This French fry shape is called a batonnet in the French kitchen.

Immediately place the batonnets into the bowl with cool water. The excess potato starch will be rinsed away. After all the fries have been rinsed, line a rimmed baking sheet with paper towels and transfer the fries to the tray. Use more towels to blot water from the top.

Set up a deep fryer with about 5 inches (12.5 cm) of oil and heat the oil to 325°F (170°C). An enamel-coated cast-iron fryer is a great choice for this, if available. Carefully use a spider to add the fries to the oil in small batches. This first fry helps create a thin crust on each fry and precooks the center. Fry for about 5 minutes. They'll still look quite pale. Have a pan with a rack to allow to drain and cool. Let the oil temperature recover to 325°F (170°C) before dropping in the next batch.

When ready to eat, heat the oil to 365°F (185°C). Drop in the fries in small batches using a spider. When the fries turn golden brown, after about 4 minutes, use the spider to gather the fries, allow to drain for a moment, then toss in the bowl with the garlic mixture. Season with salt and serve immediately with the garlic aioli.

EGGS AND BREAKFAST COOKERY

Cracking the Code for Fluffy Eggs and Other Morning Staples

I spent a lot of my early years as a short-order cook, then a breakfast cook. They say there are as many ways to cook eggs as there are folds in a chef's toque. You can spend your entire life mastering eggs and breakfast and it would be a life well spent.

Many say the egg is a perfect ingredient—well, it is definitely the most versatile. When you have no idea what to cook, if you have eggs, you're halfway to a meal. It's a protein, it's a liquid and it's also an emulsifier. In this chapter, we'll be using eggs in all those ways and more!

Along with eggs, there are other breakfast staples you need to know how to cook. What's a great breakfast repertoire without griddle favorites like French toast, pancakes and waffles? We'll teach you them all, plus more contemporary dishes, like chia pudding, which has replaced oatmeal as a morning staple. Ali makes an amazing version.

We round out the breakfast section with fun, kid-friendly creations like smoothies and breakfast tarts and add some fun tricks and tips, so enjoy these day-starting delicacies.

Spanish-Style Potato and Onion Frittata

Spain has one of my favorite omelets made from potatoes, cheese and onions called a "tortilla." Not to be confused with a Mexican tortilla, a Spanish tortilla is like the perfect mash-up of a baked potato and scrambled eggs. The Spanish serve it like an appetizer, but I love making it into an omelet. The key is to season every layer with salt and pepper at each stage. Small yellow potatoes are a bit more work to peel and dice, but they're sweeter than larger russet potatoes.

Serves 6–8

6 large eggs

Kosher salt and freshly ground pepper

½ cup (50 g) grated Parmesan, divided

1 lb (454 g) yellow potatoes, peeled and cut into small dice

4 tbsp (60 ml) extra virgin olive oil, divided, plus more for garnish

2 tbsp (28 g) unsalted butter

1 medium yellow onion, finely chopped

¼ cup (30 g) shredded mozzarella or other melting cheese

Sour cream, for serving (optional)

Preheat the oven in broiler mode and place a rack 10 to 12 inches (25 to 30.5 cm) below the heating element.

Beat the eggs in a bowl and add ½ teaspoon of salt, ¼ teaspoon of pepper and ¼ cup (25 g) of the Parmesan cheese.

Place the peeled and diced potatoes in a microwave-safe bowl, then toss with 2 tablespoons (30 ml) of the olive oil and season with ¼ teaspoon salt. Cover tightly with plastic wrap and microwave on high for 6 to 9 minutes total, or until fork tender.

Meanwhile, heat the remaining 2 tablespoons (30 ml) of olive oil and the butter over medium heat in a heavy 10-inch (25-cm) omelet pan. Add the onion and a generous pinch of salt. Cook, stirring, until tender but not browned, about 5 minutes. Add the potatoes to the pan and toss gently so that the potatoes don't break apart. Season the mixture with ½ teaspoon salt and ¼ teaspoon pepper.

Pour the reserved egg mixture into the pan over the potatoes and onions. Shake the pan gently while you lift the edges of the frittata; repeat until the eggs start to set, 2 to 3 minutes. Turn the stove to low and sprinkle the mozzarella and remaining ¼ cup (25 g) of Parmesan over the top of the frittata.

Once the frittata is mostly set, place the pan under the broiler for a minute or two to lightly brown the cheese. Remove from the heat and let the tortilla rest for at least 5 minutes. Cut into wedges and serve with some sour cream, if desired.

Fluffy and Decadent Blueberry-Ricotta Pancakes

These are our favorite pancakes because they are light and fluffy and have a fresh berry flavor. I learned this recipe while working for Chef Neal Fraser in Los Angeles. The secret is folding in whipped egg whites. The airy whites literally lift the batter and make the pancakes eat like fluffy clouds. This egg white technique can be applied to any pancake recipe.

Serves 4

3 eggs, separated

1½ cups (355 ml) milk

¼ cup (50 g) sugar

1 tbsp (15 ml) pure vanilla extract

2 cups (240 g) all-purpose flour

1 tsp baking powder

1½ tsp (9 g) kosher salt

¾ cup (185 g) ricotta cheese, drained in a coffee filter or fine sieve

¼ tsp cream of tartar (optional)

Pan spray, for the griddle

1 pint (300 g) fresh blueberries or 2 cups (300 g) frozen blueberries, thawed

Pure maple syrup, for serving

Unsalted butter, for serving

In a large bowl, whisk the egg yolks with the milk, sugar and vanilla until well combined. Add the flour, baking powder and salt. Whisk until just combined—do not overmix; small flour lumps are okay. Gently fold in the ricotta cheese until just barely combined. Again, some ricotta clumps are okay.

In a separate bowl, using an electric mixer with the whisk attachment, beat the egg whites and cream of tartar (if using) at medium speed until frothy. Then switch to high speed and beat until soft peaks form, 4 to 6 minutes. Gently fold the egg whites into the batter until just combined.

Heat a griddle over medium heat and give it a 3-second spray with pan spray to coat. Dip a 2-ounce (56-g) ladle into the batter and ladle onto the griddle. Be sure to leave enough space between the pancakes to get your spatula in there to flip. Cook over medium heat until the bottoms are golden brown and the pancakes are just beginning to set, 1 to 2 minutes. Sprinkle each pancake with a few blueberries, pressing them in gently. Flip over and continue to cook until golden on the second side. Remove from the heat and repeat with the remaining batter. Serve with maple syrup and butter.

> **Chef Tip:** You can make the batter a day ahead and keep covered in the fridge. Bring the batter to room temperature before cooking the pancakes. If making a large batch, you can keep them warm in a 180°F (82°C) oven.

Pain Perdu: French Toast with Almonds and Strawberries

Pain perdu is thick slices of bread soaked in a sweet custard, then griddled until golden brown. Bathe them in butter and you've created heaven on a plate. Maple syrup is always great, but I love making a fruit topping, especially when strawberries are in season. You can use any fruit at the peak of ripeness. This topping recipe is great for any super sweet fruit that is too soft to eat as hand fruit.

Serves 4

Strawberry Topping

1 lb (454 g) strawberries, rinsed, dried, trimmed and halved

3 tbsp (36 g) sugar

3 tbsp (45 ml) freshly squeezed lemon juice

1 tsp finely grated lemon zest

½ cup (50 g) slivered almonds, toasted

French Toast

8 slices thick Texas toast

1 cup (235 ml) half-and-half

1 cup (235 ml) milk

5 large eggs

5 tbsp (60 g) sugar

1½ tbsp (23 ml) vanilla extract

¼ tsp salt

4 tbsp (56 g) unsalted butter, divided

To make the strawberry topping, add the strawberries, sugar, lemon juice and lemon zest to a medium-size bowl. Stir until well combined and let stand for at least 30 minutes in the fridge. Stir again when ready to use.

Most slivered almonds come toasted, but to give them extra deliciousness, toast the almonds in a nonstick pan over medium heat for 1 to 2 minutes, until fragrant. Set aside.

To make the French toast, place the Texas toast in a single layer in a large baking dish with high sides. In a medium-size bowl, whisk together the half-and-half, milk, eggs, sugar, vanilla and salt for about 30 seconds, or until combined. Pour over the Texas toast in the baking dish and let settle for about 1 minute. Turn over again to coat. Let the Texas toast soak up the custard for about 3 minutes, until soaked but not falling-apart soggy. You can also do this in batches if you don't have a large baking dish.

Preheat a large nonstick skillet over medium heat for 1 to 2 minutes. Add half the butter; it should melt pretty quickly and turn a pale brown. Lift the toast out of the custard, let it drip for about a second, then gently place it into the pan. Repeat until you've filled the pan with a single layer, usually 4 slices. Let cook until golden brown, about 3 minutes. Reduce the heat to medium-low if the toast is browning too quickly. Flip over and cook on the other side for 2 to 3 minutes, until the toast is firm and bounces back when you touch it, which means the custard is cooked through. Remove from the skillet and repeat with the remaining butter and toast.

> **Chef Tip:** If you don't have a grill pan or large skillet, an electric skillet does a good job. The combination of eggs and milk or cream makes a custard that is similar to flan or an ice cream base.

The Ultimate Bacon and Egg Breakfast Sandwich

This sandwich is perfect because it's like a grilled cheese meets a breakfast sandwich! My days as a boat cook helped me perfect this breakfast favorite. I love thick-cut white bread (aka Texas toast), but I will also use a sourdough bread. As with all recipes, feel free to customize with the ingredients you like. If you don't like runny eggs, a firm scramble would taste great. Ham, Canadian bacon or even sausage would also be delicious.

Serves 1

4 thick slices cooked bacon

1 tbsp (14 g) mayonnaise

2 thick slices Texas toast or very thick white bread

2 slices cheddar cheese

4 slices tomato

2 leaves butter lettuce

1 tsp unsalted butter

1 large egg

In a skillet, warm the cooked bacon, turning, until crisp, 2 to 3 minutes. Transfer to paper towels to drain.

Spread the mayonnaise on one side of a piece of bread, then place the cheddar cheese on top. Spread the mayonnaise on the other slice of the toast, then top with the bacon, tomato and lettuce.

Heat a large, nonstick skillet over medium heat. Place both halves of the sandwich in the skillet bread-side down as it heats up. Once it starts toasting, cook for 2 to 4 minutes until golden brown. Transfer to a plate and reserve.

Return the same skillet back to medium heat, melt the butter. Add the egg and fry over medium heat, turning once, until crisp around the edges, about 4 minutes; the yolk should still be runny. Slide the egg onto the lettuce; close the sandwich and eat right away.

Chef Tip: Mayonnaise, not butter, is the best spread to get toasted bread golden brown and delicious. Mayonnaise is made mostly of oil, so it's simply the best medium to toast bread with.

Fancy Brunch Egg, Bacon and Gruyère Breakfast Tart

I love frozen puff pastry—it's instant chef cred in a box. It is light, is very flaky when baked and has a million uses, both savory and sweet. Chefs call this type of dough a laminated dough, meaning it has a lot of layers in it. The layers are made of flour, butter as the fat and water. Flour and water together make a dough, trapping butter in between the layers. Repeatedly folding it over itself and rolling it is called laminating. In a hot oven, the water in the dough evaporates and creates steam. The steam pushes up but because it's trapped, creates bubbles. Then the dough sets as it cooks, and that's how you get the layers of deliciousness.

Serves 6

1 sheet puff pastry, thawed until workable but not too warm

1 egg, beaten

1 cup (120 g) grated Gruyère cheese

½ cup (120 g) crème fraîche

Salt and freshly ground pepper, to taste

7 slices cooked bacon

4 eggs

2½ cups (50 g) arugula

2 tbsp (30 ml) olive oil

Juice from ½ lemon

⅓ cup (16 g) sliced chives

Roll out the puff pastry sheet on a lightly floured surface to make a large rectangle just smaller than a half sheet pan. Line a sheet pan with parchment paper and place the rolled puff pastry on top. Create a 1-inch (2.5-cm) border all around by scoring with a knife, similar to a picture frame. "Dock" the dough by poking holes with a fork in the center area, only leaving the border alone. Brush the border edges with the beaten egg. Refrigerate the dough for 10 minutes.

Meanwhile, mix the Gruyère cheese, crème fraîche and a pinch each of salt and pepper in a small bowl. Set aside.

Preheat the oven to 400°F (200°C).

Remove the dough from the refrigerator and spread the cheese mixture in the center rectangle of the dough. Place the bacon on top, leaving space for the eggs. Bake for 12 minutes, until the crust starts to puff and become light brown. Remove from the oven.

Now crack the eggs and place them between the bacon on the tart. Return to the oven and continue to bake for 7 to 10 minutes, until the egg whites are set and the yolks are your desired doneness. Remove from the oven.

Toss the arugula, olive oil and lemon juice in a medium-size bowl. Season with salt and pepper to taste. Garnish the tart with the arugula salad and chives. Cut into squares and serve immediately.

> **Chef Tip**: A tart is a simple term for an open-face pastry with some kind of filling. Before baking the tart, you can brush it with a "wash" to enhance its flavor and appearance. Each wash creates a different look: Whole beaten egg = extra browning with shine. Beaten egg white = shine with no extra browning (color). Milk wash = matte brown finish with no shine. And there are many more washes.

Superfood Smoothie

We know it seems mundane to make smoothies, but if you have kids you know these are not just beverages. These are vitamin, vegetable and life-giving elixirs! Like in a restaurant we utilize what's in the freezer to limit waste. There are always items like kale, baby carrots, apples, grapes, turmeric and other fruit that's prepped or hanging out. We cut it up and freeze it all so there is always a large bag full of frozen smoothie ingredients ready to go. We're not doctors, but we believe that turmeric is a magical root—it's antiseptic, anti-inflammatory, antibiotic and anti-boring! It's always on hand in our house. We buy it fresh, roughly chop it and keep it with the frozen smoothie bag.

Makes two 8-oz (224-g) smoothies

1½ cups (355 ml) sugar-free cranberry juice

1 tbsp (7 g) dry chia seeds

1 banana, peeled

2 cups (300 g) frozen fruit

¾ cup (180 g) vanilla Greek yogurt

½ cup (35 g) chopped kale

2" (5-cm) piece turmeric root or 1 tsp ground turmeric

Add all the ingredients for your desired smoothie to a blender. Blend until smooth, adding more liquid if needed to turn the blender blade. Add more ice to make your smoothies thick and frosty.

Chef Tip: Freeze all cut fruit in a quarter sheet pan overnight. Once the fruit is frozen, you can transfer it to a 1- or 2-gallon (3.6- or 7.2-L) freezer bag. We make our smoothies with all frozen fruit and no ice.

Ali's Breakfast Chilaquiles with Roasted Chile Sauce

This is a classic Mexican breakfast dish that is reminiscent of a casserole. The base layer is corn chips smothered with a rich red sauce topped with fried or over-easy eggs. It's one of Ali's favorite dishes to eat and cook. Making a rich red sauce from dried chiles is easier than you think. All the rich, deep, sweet flavors are in the chiles. The secret to coaxing out the layers contained in the essential oils is to seed the chiles and then toast them until fragrant.

Serves 4

1 (4-oz [112-g]) package dried guajillo chiles (8–9 chiles)

1 cup (235 ml) warm water

1 (15-oz [420-g]) can diced tomatoes, with juice

3 cloves garlic

3 tbsp (45 ml) canola oil

3 cups (705 ml) chicken stock, homemade (page 107) or store-bought

1 tsp kosher salt

½ tsp sugar

8–10 cups (320–400 g) restaurant-style tortilla chips

4 eggs, sunny-side up, or as you prefer

½ onion, very thinly shaved on a mandoline

1 cup (120 g) grated Mexican cheese, such as Ranchero or queso fresco

½ cup (120 g) sour cream

¼ cup (10 g) roughly chopped fresh cilantro

Cut open the chiles with scissors to remove the seeds and stems. Toast in a dry, heavy pan over high heat until aromatic and well toasted, but not burnt, 2 to 4 minutes. Place the chiles in a medium-size bowl and cover with the warm water. Keep them weighted down with a large plate for about 30 minutes to reconstitute.

Drain the chiles, reserving the soaking liquid. Place the chiles, tomatoes, garlic and ¾ cup (180 ml) of the soaking liquid in a blender. Blend until smooth and even, then strain through a sieve.

Heat the oil in a Dutch oven over medium-high heat. At the first wisp of white smoke, add the puréed chile mixture and cook, stirring constantly, until the consistency of tomato paste, about 2 minutes. Stir in the chicken stock, salt and sugar and allow to come to a boil. Reduce the heat to a low simmer and cook, loosely covered with a lid, for 20 minutes. Remove from the heat and set aside.

When ready to eat, preheat the oven to 350°F (180°C).

Place the chips on a parchment-lined sheet pan and bake for 4 to 6 minutes, until fragrant. Gently fold the chips into the sauce until lightly but evenly coated. Separate the chips into 4 equal servings. Place the fried eggs on top of the chips and garnish with the onion, Mexican cheese, sour cream and cilantro.

> **Chef Tip:** Not all tortilla chips are the same. Store-bought brands are flimsy. Try to find thick "restaurant style" chips if you have a local Mexican market, or cut corn tortillas and fry them for this dish.

Ali's Coconut Chia Pudding with Almonds and Fresh Berries

The chia plant is actually related to mint. The seeds, when soaked, gelatinize and get chewy like tapioca. What we love about chia pudding is, it's like eating dessert for breakfast. It tastes and feels like tapioca pudding. It has a nice refreshing creaminess from the fresh coconut milk. This is Ali's go-to chia pudding recipe that we know you're going to love!

Serves 4–6

½ cup (60 g) sliced almonds

2 cups (470 ml) vanilla-flavored almond milk

½ cup (56 g) chia seeds

1½ tsp (8 ml) vanilla extract

¾ cup (120 g) coconut cream (if you can't find coconut cream, use coconut milk)

½ cup (160 g) honey, for drizzling

1 cup (150 g) fresh assorted berries

½ cup (40) shredded sweetened coconut

Preheat the oven to 350°F (180°C).

Place the almonds in an even layer on a baking sheet lined with foil or parchment paper. Toast in the oven for 7 to 9 minutes, or until they're fragrant and golden. Watch them carefully, so they don't burn. Remove from the oven.

In a medium-size bowl, whisk together the almond milk, chia seeds and vanilla. Let the mixture stand for 30 to 40 minutes at room temperature to allow it to thicken. Whisk the seeds midway through to prevent clumping. The seeds will swell, gelatinize and begin to resemble mini tapioca pearls.

Whisk in the coconut cream and break up any clumps of seeds. Cover the chia mixture with plastic wrap and refrigerate until thickened or overnight.

Spoon the pudding into 4 to 6 bowls. Drizzle the honey over the surface of the pudding. Garnish with the berries, almonds and coconut. Serve and enjoy!

Chef Tip: You can use white or black chia seeds. If using coconut milk, use one that doesn't have sugar in it; that other stuff is used to make drinks.

Classic Eggs Benedict and Blender Hollandaise

Every cook should know how to poach eggs and make a hollandaise sauce. Both are not easy but well worth the time learning. Take your time and organize. This recipe will teach coordination, organization and good mise en place. Read through the recipe and understand how all the components work together. Hollandaise is one of the five French mother sauces. It's called a mother sauce because it can be served as is or, with a few add-ins, become other sauces. Hollandaise usually is made by hand whisking, which takes forever, and the coordination of whisking while streaming the butter can be difficult. It's kind of like rubbing your belly while tapping your head. The result is usually disastrous and a pain to do. This recipe makes it easy by using the blender as the whisk.

Serves 4

Blender Hollandaise Sauce
1 cup (225 g) unsalted butter

6 large egg yolks, at room temperature

3 tbsp (45 ml) freshly squeezed lemon juice

2 tsp (10 ml) water

1 tsp salt

3 dashes hot sauce (such as Tabasco), or to taste (optional)

Eggs Benedict
8 slices Canadian bacon or ham

4 English muffins, fork split, toasted

3 tbsp (42 g) unsalted butter, softened

8 poached eggs

Maldon salt, for garnish

Paprika, for garnish (optional)

To make the hollandaise sauce, melt the butter in a small saucepan over medium heat, or in the microwave, and set aside. Place the yolks, lemon juice, water, salt and hot sauce into a blender. Turn the blender to medium speed. While running, slowly stream in the melted butter; you'll start to see the hollandaise thicken and turn a pale yellow color.

Turn off the blender and check the consistency. If it's still on the thin side, like a salad dressing, pulse on the highest speed for about 5 seconds at a time. Once you achieve the thickness of chocolate syrup, taste and adjust the seasoning if necessary. Keep the sauce warm over a slowly simmering double boiler while you prepare the rest of the dish.

To make the eggs Benedict, warm the Canadian bacon or ham slices in a skillet over medium heat. Toast the English muffins and apply butter to both sides. Hold until ready to assemble.

Working quickly, poach the eggs. As the eggs poach (within 4 minutes), place 2 toasted English muffin halves on each of 4 plates. Place the warm Canadian bacon or ham slices on each half of the English muffins, so each is ready for its egg. When the eggs are done, remove from the water with a slotted spoon, dab on a towel to remove excess water, place an egg on each English muffin with ham and cover each with the warm hollandaise. Garnish with Maldon salt and paprika. Serve immediately.

Chef Tip: An emulsion is getting two liquids that would usually not bond together to combine into a thick sauce by using an emulsifier. In this sauce, the egg yolk is the emulsifier that holds the butter and lemon juice in a thick suspension.

Variation: Sauce Maltese
Include the juice and zest of an orange or a blood orange with the yolks, lemon juice, water and salt and substitute freshly ground pepper for the hot sauce before running the blender.

Jet's Famous Fried Chicken and Waffles

Southern in origin, chicken and waffles is a hearty meal that satisfies people's love for sweet and salty. Crispy, salty fried chicken with sweet and buttery waffles is a magical pair. Feel free to swap in your favorite maple syrup and hot sauce. My favorite combo is pure maple syrup and Sriracha.

Serves 4

Chicken
4 (4–6-oz [112–168-g]) boneless chicken breasts or thighs
1 tbsp (15 g) seasoned salt
2 cups (470 ml) buttermilk

Breading
2 cups (240 g) all-purpose flour
1½ tsp (8 g) seasoned salt
1 cup (115 g) panko bread crumbs

3–4 quarts (2.7–3.6 L) oil, for frying

To Serve
4 Crispy and Fluffy Waffles (page 171)
Unsalted butter, softened
Maple syrup
Homemade Sriracha (page 171)

To make the chicken, take a heavy-duty zip-top bag and cut open one side of it. Place the chicken pieces in the bag, leaving it slightly open so as not to create an air bubble. Using a small frying pan or rolling pin, pound into even ¼-inch (6-mm) thick pieces. Place the pounded chicken in a medium-size bowl, sprinkle with the seasoned salt and pour in the buttermilk. Cover with plastic wrap and marinate in the fridge for 4 hours and up to overnight.

To make the breading, in a large bowl, combine the flour, seasoned salt and bread crumbs, and stir until well mixed.

When ready to fry, heat the oil in a heavy skillet until 360°F (182°C) on a frying thermometer. Remove the chicken from the buttermilk, but do not shake off the excess buttermilk. Place the marinated chicken into the breading mix and press the breading into the chicken. Press both sides in the breading and shake off the excess. Carefully place the chicken in the oil and fry 3 to 5 minutes, until cooked through or the internal temperature reaches 160°F (71°C) in the thickest part of each piece. Remove from the oil with a slotted spoon and drain on a paper towel–lined plate.

To serve, place the fried chicken on top of the cooked waffles. Top with butter, maple syrup and Sriracha.

*See photo on page 170.

Chef Tip: You can substitute chicken thighs or even whole pieces of chicken in the recipe. You can double the breading and use it to fry up one whole fried chicken cut into 8 pieces.

Crispy and Fluffy Waffles

We love waffles because they are crisp, light and satisfying. You can make these waffles ahead, freeze them and reheat them in a 350°F (180°C) oven. You can also substitute buttermilk in the batter to get very crispy waffles. The acid in the buttermilk gives a nice tang and reacts with the baking powder, making for airier waffles.

Makes 4–6 waffles

2 eggs

2 cups (240 g) all-purpose flour

1¾ cups (415 ml) milk

½ cup (120 ml) vegetable oil

1 tbsp (12 g) sugar

4 tsp (20 g) baking powder

¼ tsp salt

1½ tsp (8 ml) vanilla extract

Pan spray

Preheat a waffle iron to 400°F (200°C).

In a large bowl using a hand mixer or a stand mixer with the whisk attachment, beat the eggs until fluffy. Add the flour, milk, vegetable oil, sugar, baking powder, salt and vanilla and beat just until smooth. Transfer the batter to a 4-cup (960-ml) measuring cup to make it easy to pour.

Spray the preheated waffle iron with pan spray. Pour the batter onto the hot waffle iron and cook until golden brown, following the manufacturer's instructions. Serve hot.

Homemade Sriracha

Did you know Sriracha is not just a sauce but also a town in Thailand that grows amazing chiles? The bottle with the green cap and roosters on the label is not authentic Sriracha. This recipe from my first book has a more balanced flavor and is a little sweet, savory and not too acidic, like the real deal.

Makes about 2 cups (470 ml)

12 oz (340 g) red jalapeños, stems removed and roughly chopped

4 oz (112 g) red serranos, stems removed and roughly chopped

8 oz (224 g) green jalapeños, stems removed and roughly chopped

4 cloves garlic

2 tbsp (25 g) granulated sugar

2 tbsp (30 g) brown sugar

1–2 tsp (6–12 g) salt

½ cup (120 ml) distilled white vinegar

1 tsp xanthan gum

Place the peppers, garlic, both sugars and salt in a food processor and pulse until roughly chopped. Transfer the mixture to a clean container, cover and let sit at room temperature. A mason jar with a loose-fitting lid or a clean bowl with plastic wrap will work. Fermentation should begin in about 2 days. When bubbles begin to form, stir your "mash" once or twice a day to combine and help settle. Continue until the mixture stops bubbling, 6 to 8 days.

Transfer the mash to a blender, add the vinegar and purée until very smooth. Strain the sauce through a fine sieve. Add the xanthan gum and purée again until smooth and thick. Store your sauce in squeeze bottles in the fridge for up to 3 months.

Chef Tip: If you love really spicy Sriracha, reverse the proportions of the serrano and jalapeños. And if you think that's not going to be hot enough for you, substitute the chiles for Scotch bonnets and Thai chiles. I'm not responsible for the burning of your mouth or bottom if you go this route!

DESSERTS

Not Your Average Cakes, Pies and Other Beloved Sweets

Ali is the dessert chef in this house, and she has put together a great group of recipes to satisfy your sweet tooth. Some of these recipes will be on the tougher side to make, but remember to stay with it and practice. We'll be covering a lot of the classics by category.

Custards seem so benign, but oh the things you can make with the humble beginnings of eggs, cream and sugar! From custards, we'll be making ice cream, bread pudding and anglaise sauces.

You can't have a dessert section without chocolate. We'll be making dipping sauces, swirling it into banana bread and making peanut butter and chocolate tarts. We'll make a few types of doughs, too. Pies, quick breads and soufflés are just a few examples.

Some desserts have multiple parts, so we recommend you read a recipe all the way through before starting. It will help you organize and plan. Most of all, have fun with these recipes and take your time. It will be well worth it.

Shiny Glazed Chocolate Cake with Raspberries and Raspberry Sauce

I love this cake. Why? It's simple, yet it feels rich and indulgent. Plus, it's a showstopper with its mirrored chocolate glaze and fresh raspberry sauce. I was taught this beautiful glaze by pastry master Jim Dodge. While there are many different types of cakes to choose from, we're making a chocolate cake that will get part of its rise by creaming butter and sugar together. This creates structure by working tiny air bubbles into the butter and sugar mixture. A little baking powder will give it the rest of the rise. Make sure the glaze is at the correct temperature to avoid a coating that's too thin.

Serves 8–10

Chocolate Cake
¾ cup (170 g) unsalted butter, softened but not greasy, plus melted butter for the pan

1½ cups plus 1 tbsp (190 g) cake flour, plus more for the pan

½ cup (50 g) cocoa powder

2½ tsp (10 g) baking powder

4 oz (112 g) unsweetened chocolate

1½ cups plus 2 tbsp (325 g) sugar

1 tsp salt

4 eggs

1¼ cups (295 ml) milk

Shiny Chocolate Glaze
9 oz (255 g) good-quality unsalted butter

9 oz (255 g) dark chocolate (about 62% cacao), chopped

Preheat the oven to 350°F (180°C).

To make the cake, trace the bottom of a 9-inch (23-cm) cake pan onto a piece of parchment paper and cut out the circle. Using a pastry brush, brush the inside of the cake pan with melted butter and place the parchment round on the bottom. Brush the parchment with melted butter and flour the entire inside of the cake pan. Whisk together the cake flour, cocoa powder and baking powder in a medium-size bowl until combined. Melt the chocolate in a heatproof bowl set over a pan of simmering water or a double boiler. Set aside to cool slightly.

Place the butter, sugar and salt in the bowl of a stand mixer fitted with the paddle attachment. Cream together on medium-high speed until the butter is fluffy and lightened in color, 6 to 8 minutes, scraping down the sides and bottom of the bowl occasionally. (Creaming butter and sugar helps incorporate air and gives your cake good structure.)

Add the melted chocolate and mix on low speed until incorporated. Add the eggs one at a time and mix on low speed until combined. Alternate adding the milk and the flour mixture to the batter, one-third at a time, mixing on low speed until just incorporated. Do not overmix the batter.

Pour the cake batter into the prepared pan. Spin the pan so the batter grips slightly to the sides. This helps prevent the cake from forming a dome on top. Bake the cake for 50 minutes to 1 hour, until a toothpick inserted into the center comes out clean with a few moist crumbs sticking to it and the cake has pulled slightly away from the sides. Cool the cake completely on a cooling rack in the pan. Wrapped tightly in plastic, the cake can be stored in the refrigerator for up to 1 week or in the freezer for up to 1 month.

To make the glaze, melt the butter and chocolate in a heatproof bowl set over a pan of simmering water or a double boiler. Stir until it's smooth. Cool the chocolate and butter to about 83°F (28°C).

(continued)

Raspberry Sauce

4 cups (500 g) raspberries, rinsed and picked through

½ cup (100 g) sugar

1 tbsp (15 ml) freshly squeezed lemon juice

4 tsp (10 g) cornstarch

½ cup (120 ml) cold water

2 (6-oz [170-g]) packages raspberries, for garnish

To make the raspberry sauce, in a medium-size saucepan over medium heat, combine the raspberries, sugar and lemon juice. Crush the raspberries with a spoon as you stir the mixture, bringing it almost to a boil, 3 to 5 minutes. Remember to taste the sauce and adjust the lemon or sugar based on the sweetness of the raspberries. Strain the mixture through a strainer into a medium-size bowl, pushing on the solids. In a small bowl, combine the cornstarch and cold water to make a slurry. Return the raspberry sauce to the pan. Add the slurry and simmer over low heat until the sauce thickens, about 5 minutes. Set aside to cool.

Run a paring knife around the edge between the cake and the pan, trying not to cut the sides of the cake. Carefully turn the cake out of the cake pan and peel off the parchment paper. If the cake has a dome on the top, carefully trim it from the cake as level as possible. I like to invert the cake and glaze the bottom to get the most level top to the cake. Place a piece of parchment paper in a sheet pan, then a cooling rack over it. Lay an 8-inch (20-cm) cake pan upside down on the cooling rack. Place the inverted cake on the overturned pan and pour the glaze in a steady stream starting in the center of the cake, moving to the outer edges in a clockwise motion. Be sure to save enough glaze to coat the sides of the cake. Allow the glaze to run off the cake and, with a paring knife, smooth any drips from the bottom edge. Before the glaze sets, place the raspberries for garnish in a circle along the top edge of the cake.

The cake can be served as soon as the glaze sets or refrigerated for a few hours to a day, covered in the refrigerator. Slice into wedges and serve with the raspberry sauce.

> **Chef Tip:** Lightly sweep a kitchen torch on low over the chocolate glaze to restore the original shininess.

Best-Ever Chocolate Swirl Banana Bread

Few things are as comforting as a warm, freshly baked slice of banana bread, a buttery, banana-y, toasty pecan loaf of goodness! Banana bread is a quick bread, which basically means it doesn't require any fermentation (rise) like a yeasted bread. We're adding a chocolate swirl to this traditional quick bread because . . . chocolate! Be sure to use overripe bananas, the darker the skin the better, to ensure maximum sweetness.

Makes 1 loaf

½ cup (112 g) unsalted butter, melted, plus more for the pan

½ cup (60 g) pecans

1½ cups (180 g) all-purpose flour

½ tsp ground cinnamon

⅛ tsp ground nutmeg

½ tsp salt

1¼ cups (280 g) smashed, overripe bananas

1 cup (200 g) sugar

2 eggs

1 tsp vanilla extract

½ cup (120 g) sour cream

3½ oz (100 g) semisweet chocolate, roughly chopped

Preheat the oven to 350°F (180°C). Butter the sides of a 9 x 5–inch (23 x 12.5–cm) loaf pan and set it aside.

Spread the pecans on a baking sheet lined with foil or parchment paper. Roast them in the oven for 10 minutes, until fragrant and lightly toasted. Allow the pecans to cool, then chop them and set them aside.

In a medium-size bowl, whisk together the flour, cinnamon, nutmeg and salt until well combined.

Place the bananas in the bowl of a stand mixer fitted with the paddle attachment. Mix for about a minute to smash the bananas thoroughly, then add the melted butter and mix until incorporated. Add the sugar and mix until combined. Add the eggs and vanilla and mix until combined. Finally, add the flour mixture and mix until just combined. Do not overmix the batter, which can make the crumb tough and result in large "worm" holes. Using a spatula, gently fold in the pecans and sour cream until just incorporated.

Melt the chopped chocolate in a heatproof bowl set over a pan of simmering water or a double boiler. Allow the chocolate to cool slightly. In a medium-size bowl, mix 1 cup (235 ml) of the batter with the chocolate until well combined.

Pour one-third of the banana batter into the prepared pan. Drop two large spoonfuls of the chocolate batter side by side in the center of the batter. Cover this with another third of the banana batter followed by the remaining chocolate batter. Cover this with the last third of the banana batter. Using a knife, swirl the two batters through the loaf pan a few times, without overmixing.

Transfer to the oven and bake for 50 to 55 minutes, until a toothpick inserted into the center of the bread comes out clean (okay, there may be a crumb. Or two). Allow the loaf to cool in the pan for 5 minutes, then transfer to a cooling rack to continue cooling, and you're done! Boom. Banana chocolate deliciousness.

Chef Tip: This recipe uses the muffin method: mixing the wet ingredients together, the dry ingredients together, then combining both the wet and the dry ingredients, finished by folding in the sour cream and pecans.

Peanut Butter Cup Tart with Chocolate Cookie Crust

Peanut butter cups are iconic. They're a childhood favorite for Ali. Okay, who are we kidding—they're an adult favorite, too! So, I'm taking this classic flavor combination and creating a tart. Sweet peanut butter filling inside a chocolate cookie crust with a chocolate ganache topping makes a grown-up peanut butter cup.

Makes one 9-inch (23-cm) tart

Chocolate Cookie Crust
1½ cups (170 g) chocolate wafer cookie crumbs

¼ tsp salt

6 tbsp (84 g) unsalted butter, melted

Peanut Butter Filling
1¼ cups (325 g) chunky peanut butter

5 tbsp (70 g) unsalted butter, softened

¾ cup (90 g) confectioners' sugar

¼ tsp salt

¼ tsp ground nutmeg

2 tbsp (30 ml) whole milk, or more as needed

1½ tsp (8 ml) vanilla extract

Chocolate Ganache Topping
5 oz (142 g) good-quality semisweet chocolate, roughly chopped

⅓ cup (80 ml) heavy cream

2 tbsp (28 g) unsalted butter

1½ tbsp (23 ml) light corn syrup

¾ cup (110 g) chopped roasted, salted peanuts, for garnish

Preheat the oven to 350°F (180°C).

To make the crust, in a medium-size bowl, mix the chocolate wafer cookie crumbs and salt. Add the melted butter and mix until the cookie crumbs are well coated. Sprinkle the cookie crumb mixture in a 9-inch (23-cm) tart pan, with a little extra around the base of the sides. Press the crumbs on the bottom and sides of the pan using the heel of your hand or a tart tamper. Make sure the crust is as even in thickness as possible. Blind bake the crust for 8 to 10 minutes, then place it on a wire rack and allow it to cool completely. (Blind baking means to partially or fully cook a pie or tart crust that has a filling that is cooked for only a short period of time or not at all.)

To make the peanut butter filling, in a stand mixer fitted with the paddle attachment, beat the peanut butter and softened butter until well mixed. Add the confectioners' sugar, salt and nutmeg and mix to combine. Next, add the milk and vanilla extract and beat until smooth, about 1 minute. Fill the cooled crust with the peanut butter filling, leveling it with an offset spatula. The crust should extend above the filling slightly to leave space for the chocolate ganache topping.

To make the chocolate ganache topping, melt the chocolate in a heatproof bowl set over a pan of simmering water or a double boiler. Whisk in the heavy cream until smooth. Add the butter and corn syrup and whisk until the butter is melted and the chocolate mixture is smooth. Pour the chocolate mixture on top of the tart, moving the tart in a tilting motion so the chocolate runs to the sides and covers the entire top of the tart. Garnish the edges of the tart with the chopped peanuts. Refrigerate the tart for at least 1 hour and serve chilled. The tart can be made 1 day ahead and stored, covered, in the refrigerator.

Chef Tip: When you store the tart in the fridge, the chocolate ganache top turns opaque. Lightly sweep a kitchen torch set to low over the ganache to shine up the chocolate before serving.

Burnt Milk Ice Cream

Neither one of us can ever say no to a cool, creamy bowl of ice cream. Ice cream is technically a custard, which is simply the combination of eggs, milk or cream and sugar. Other desserts that are custards are flan, anglaise, crème brûlée and more! When you bring up the temperature of whipped eggs, they thicken (coagulate) and trap air bubbles, which make that airy, creamy texture in food. This stirred, stovetop custard utilizes a crème anglaise base. Although this is a burnt milk recipe, the amounts are similar to a basic vanilla ice cream. Once you've mastered basic vanilla, you can use that as a base for other flavors.

Makes 2 quarts (1.8 L)

4⅓ cups (1 L) milk

3 cups (705 ml) heavy cream

2 tsp (10 g) vanilla bean paste or (10 ml) vanilla extract

1 tsp salt

1¼ cups (250 g) sugar, divided

4 eggs

Variations

Vanilla Ice Cream: Follow the same recipe for the burnt milk, omitting the first step of burning the milk and only using 3¾ cups (898 ml) of milk. You can increase the amount of vanilla bean paste/extract if you like.

Green Tea Ice Cream: Follow the recipe for the Vanilla Ice Cream above and whisk in 4 tablespoons (16 g) of matcha green tea powder when whisking the eggs and sugar before tempering.

Place the milk in a small pot over high heat and burn it intentionally. Yep, you heard that right. You want the milk solids at the bottom to burn and give it a nice charred flavor. You should end up with about 3¾ cups (898 ml) of burnt milk from evaporation during boiling. Steep the milk in the burned milk solids for 15 minutes.

Prepare a large bowl of ice for an ice bath and set it aside. Add the 3¾ cups (898 ml) of burnt milk, heavy cream, vanilla paste, salt and ½ cup (100 g) of the sugar to the pot. Bring the mixture just to a boil. While the mixture is heating, whisk the eggs and remaining ¾ cup (150 g) of sugar in a medium-size bowl until well combined. Be sure to whisk them together quickly. Sugar, if left sitting in the eggs, can crystalize and seize up, making it impossible to mix together.

Just as the milk/cream mixture barely begins to boil, remove the pot from the heat and begin tempering your eggs. Add the hot cream mixture to the eggs one ladle at a time and whisk vigorously to raise the temperature of the eggs without curdling them. Repeat this until you've incorporated half the cream mixture into the eggs. Add the egg mixture back to the pot and turn the heat down to medium-low. Cook while whisking until it reaches 170°F (77°C) on a candy thermometer. Once it reaches 170°F (77°C), it will be thick enough to coat the back of a spoon. Test it by dipping a wide wooden spoon and dragging your finger through the middle. It should leave a solid trail.

Remove the custard from the heat and strain it through a sieve into a large bowl set over the ice bath to cool. Once it is cool, place it in a covered container in the refrigerator for 12 hours (but no more than 24 hours). The custard should cool to 40°F (4°C) before spinning it in an ice cream maker.

Transfer the custard to an ice cream maker and spin it. Spin times will vary from machine to machine. Your ice cream is done spinning when it holds its shape when scooped with a spoon, but still falls a little. It should resemble soft serve at this point. Transfer the ice cream to a container with a lid and freeze it until it hardens, 2 to 3 hours.

Chef Tips: The colder the ice cream base is, the creamier the ice cream will be. Also chill your ice cream maker bowl as cold as possible before spinning.

Classic Apple Pie

Apple pie is probably the most popular American pie in history. There are two main types of pie dough: flaky pie dough and mealy (more crumbly and compact) pie dough. They both use the same recipe, but the difference is the way the fat is cut into the flour. Mealy pie dough recipes blend the butter into the flour until the dough resembles a coarse cornmeal or bread crumbs, resulting in a tender yet more crumbly/compact crust, which is better for a liquid or custard filling. Flaky pie dough recipes, which we're using here, blend the butter into the flour until it's the size of hazelnuts. Once rolled, the dough becomes a sheet, layering flakes of dough and pockets of butter (a good choice for cooked fillings or fillings with less liquid). Ali's favorite way to "cut" the butter into the dough is a stand mixer. She learned this technique from Sherry Yard and it makes a perfect flaky dough every time. If you choose to use a food processor instead, just be cautious how far you blend the butter—you may end up with a mealy pie dough instead.

Makes one 9-inch (23-cm) pie

Flaky Pie Dough
½ cup (120 ml) cold water

2 tsp (10 ml) apple cider vinegar

2½ cups (300 g) all-purpose flour

4 tsp (15 g) granulated sugar

1 tsp salt

1 cup (225 g) cold unsalted butter, cut into ½" (1.3-cm) pieces

Apple Filling
2½ lb (1.1 kg) Granny Smith apples, peeled, cored and cut into 10 wedges each

2 tbsp (30 ml) freshly squeezed lemon juice

1 tsp ground cinnamon

⅛ tsp ground nutmeg

¼ tsp salt

½ cup (100 g) granulated sugar

½ cup (112 g) packed brown sugar

4 tbsp (35 g) cornstarch

3 tbsp (45 g) unsalted butter, cut into ½" (1.3-cm) pieces

1 egg

1 tbsp (15 ml) milk

½ cup (100 g) demerara, turbinado or granulated sugar, for sprinkling

To make the dough, mix the water and apple cider vinegar in a small bowl. Set aside in your refrigerator to chill (the colder, the better!). Whisk together the flour, granulated sugar and salt in the bowl of a stand mixer fitted with paddle attachment. Add the cold butter and mix on low speed (so the flour doesn't fly up into your face and ruin your hair) until the butter pieces are about the size of hazelnuts, about 30 seconds. If any larger pieces of butter remain, mix in 15-second increments until the size of hazelnuts. Add the water and apple cider vinegar mixture while mixing on low speed just until the dough comes together into a ball. The dough should not be dry or crumbly, but just slightly sticky. If it still seems dry, add more water 1 tablespoon (15 ml) at a time. Gather the dough on your work surface, divide it into 2 equal parts and form them into disks. Wrap them in plastic and refrigerate for 1 hour. Have a cup of coffee, drink some wine or check your emails.

On a lightly floured surface, using a lightly floured rolling pin, roll one disk of the dough into a 12-inch (30.5-cm) round. Run your hand over the dough to make sure it's even in thickness. Gather the dough by rolling it up and over the rolling pin or by folding it into quarters and place it in a 9-inch (23-cm) pie tin. Trim the edges flush with the outer edge of the pie tin. Refrigerate it for 30 minutes while you make the filling.

To make the filling, combine the apples, lemon juice, cinnamon, nutmeg, salt, both sugars and cornstarch in a large bowl and toss so the apples are fully coated. Remove the pie tin from the refrigerator and fill it with the apple mixture. You want to really pile the apples as high and evenly as possible. Pour any remaining juices and sugar from the bowl on top of the apples. Distribute the butter pieces on top of the apples.

(continued)

Classic Apple Pie (Continued)

Grab the second half of the dough from the refrigerator and roll it into another 12-inch (30.5-cm) round. Cover the pie with it and then trim the dough, leaving 1 inch (2.5 cm) hanging over the outer edge of the pie. Gently fold this under the edge of the bottom pie crust. Crimp the edges decoratively. Cut 3 steam vents in the top of the pie. Get creative here. Use some small cookie cutters with the shape of your choice to cut the vents. Or cut shapes from leftover pieces of dough and use them to decorate the pie. If you really feel inspired, try a lattice top.

Beat the egg in a small bowl and add the milk to make an egg wash. Using a pastry brush, gently brush the outside of the pie with the egg wash and sprinkle it with the demerara sugar. Refrigerate the pie for 15 minutes, but do not allow the apple mixture to sit in the unbaked pie for more than 30 minutes. Otherwise, you may end up with a soggy crust.

Preheat your oven to 425°F (220°C) with a sheet pan in the middle of the oven.

Carefully place a piece of parchment paper on the hot sheet pan from the oven. Place the pie on the sheet pan and bake for 20 minutes. Turn the oven temperature down to 375°F (190°C) and bake until the pie is golden and the filling is bubbling, about 40 more minutes. Check the browning on the pie periodically. If it is browning too quickly, tent the pie with a piece of foil to prevent the top from burning. Don't forget to cut me a slice!

Chef Tips: Remember that crust is not just a vessel for filling but also an opportunity for flavor. Consider creating greater complexity of flavors in your crust by substituting part or all of the liquid in your dough with liquids that are complementary to your filling. For example, use Applejack or bourbon in your apple pie dough.

Keep in mind that the egg creates a shiny surface on pastry while the milk creates the browning effect. You can always substitute water for the milk if your pastries tend to brown too much or too quickly.

Churros with Mexican Chocolate Dipping Sauce

The base for the beloved churro is pâte choux. Pâte choux is technically a thick paste made from a roux with the addition of eggs. Pâte choux is a versatile base. When baked, it makes cream puffs, éclairs and cheese puffs. Cooked in water, it makes gnocchi. In this recipe, we'll fry it to make churros.

Makes 8–10 churros

Mexican Chocolate Dipping Sauce

1½ cups (225 g) chopped dark chocolate

¼ cup (60 ml) heavy cream

⅓ cup (68 g) sugar

⅓ cup (80 ml) water

¼ cup (56 g) unsalted butter, at room temperature

½ cup (120 g) sour cream

1 tbsp (8 g) ancho chile powder

Cinnamon Sugar

1 cup (200 g) sugar

1 tbsp (8 g) ground cinnamon

½ tsp salt

Churros

½ cup (112 g) unsalted butter

½ tsp salt

1 cup (235 ml) water

1 tsp vanilla extract

1 tbsp (12 g) sugar

1 cup (120 g) all-purpose flour

3 large eggs

10–12 cups (2.4–2.7 L) canola oil, for frying

To make the sauce, melt the chocolate in a heatproof bowl set over a pan of simmering water or a double boiler. Set the chocolate aside. Heat the heavy cream, sugar and water in a medium-size pan over medium-high heat until just boiling. Pour the hot cream mixture over the melted chocolate and mix until well combined. Stir in the butter while the ganache is still warm. Mix in the sour cream and ancho chile powder until the chocolate sauce is smooth. Cover the sauce and set aside.

To make the cinnamon sugar, in a small bowl, whisk together the sugar, cinnamon and salt. Sprinkle it on a large plate for rolling the churros.

To make the churros, in a medium-size saucepan over high heat, combine the butter, salt, water, vanilla and sugar. Bring to a boil, then turn the heat to low. Stir in the flour. Continue stirring with a wooden spoon for about 30 seconds until the dough comes together and no lumps remain. It should form a ball and resemble mashed potatoes. Transfer the dough to the bowl of a stand mixer fitted with the paddle attachment. Start the mixer at medium speed to allow the dough to cool slightly. Add the eggs, one at a time, while mixing on medium-low speed, scraping the sides of the bowl occasionally. Make sure the eggs are fully incorporated before adding the next egg. The dough may look broken, but that's okay. It will come together as you keep beating. Beat in the last egg until the dough is glossy and sticky. Transfer the dough to a piping bag fitted with a closed star tip. (I like to use a 0.69-inch [1.8-cm] closed star tip to pipe churros. A closed star will create more pronounced ridges in your churro, but an open star or plain tip works, too!)

Fill a large pot about 6 inches (15 cm) high with the canola oil and heat it to 365 to 370°F (185 to 188°C). Pipe the churros straight into the oil—be careful, it's hot!—until they are 4 to 6 inches (10 to 15 cm) long. Use a paring knife or scissors to cut the dough from the piping tip. If you feel uneasy about piping into hot oil, or you like a perfectly straight churro, you can pipe your churros onto a parchment-lined sheet pan and freeze them for 30 minutes before frying. Fry 3 churros at a time until golden brown, turning them occasionally, about 8 to 10 minutes. Remember that the temperature of the oil will decrease when you add the churros. Try to keep it at a stable 365 to 370°F (185 to 188°C) while frying for the best results. Drain the churros on paper towels or a cooling rack set over a sheet pan for a few minutes before rolling them in the cinnamon sugar. Serve warm with the chocolate sauce for dipping.

Da Bomb Budino: Italian Salted Caramel Pudding

What is a budino, you ask? A budino is an Italian pudding or custard. It's a silky, creamy, sweet dessert. We would share a version of this budino on some of our first dates at Jar restaurant in Los Angeles. Ali loved it so much she created her own version. The method for budino is very similar to a pastry cream. It is a deliciously flavored cream thickened with eggs. It eats like a non-frozen ice cream because the method is similar. Once you've mastered this recipe, you can make pastry cream and ice cream in a snap. I love pairing this budino with a caramel sauce and adding toasted almonds for a crunchy texture.

Serves 6

½ cup (60 g) toasted sliced almonds

Budino
1½ cups (355 ml) whole milk
1½ cups (355 ml) heavy cream
¾ cup (165 g) packed brown sugar
¾ cup (180 ml) water
1½ tsp (9 g) salt
5 egg yolks
¼ cup (35 g) cornstarch
3 tbsp (45 g) unsalted butter
1 tbsp (15 ml) rum

Preheat the oven to 350°F (180°C). Place the almonds on a parchment-lined sheet pan and toast in the oven until fragrant and slightly golden, 8 to 10 minutes.

To make the budino, mix the milk and heavy cream in a medium-size saucepan, bring to a simmer and set aside. Place the brown sugar, water and salt in a separate medium-size pot over medium-high heat. Bring to a boil over high heat and cook until it caramelizes and reaches 225 to 230°F (107 to 110°C) on a candy thermometer, about 10 minutes. Turn off the heat, CAREFULLY add a ladle of the hot milk and cream mixture and whisk. The cream and caramel mixture will boil up rapidly. Wait until it boils down before adding the rest of the milk and cream. Once all of the milk and cream has been added, bring the mixture back to a boil and whisk to fully dissolve the caramelized sugar, 3 to 4 minutes.

While the caramel is boiling, prepare a large bowl of ice for an ice bath and set it aside. Whisk the egg yolks and cornstarch in a medium-size bowl until well combined, making sure that no lumps remain. Once the caramel mixture is boiling, temper your eggs by adding the hot caramel mixture to the egg yolks one ladle at a time. Whisk vigorously to raise the temperature of the eggs without curdling them. Repeat this until you've incorporated half the caramel mixture into the eggs. Add the egg mixture to the pot and turn the heat down to medium-low.

Cook the mixture while constantly whisking until it's thick and just comes to a boil, about 2 minutes. You want to cook it enough so the starch cooks all the way through, but doesn't overcook and create lumps. Remove it from the heat and strain through a sieve into a large bowl. Stir in the butter and the rum until fully combined. Place the bowl over the large bowl of ice (the ice bath) and stir until cool.

(continued)

Caramel Sauce

1 cup (235 ml) heavy cream

½ tsp vanilla extract

¼ cup (60 ml) corn syrup

1 cup (200 g) granulated sugar

¼ cup (60 ml) water

½ tsp salt

¼ cup (56 g) unsalted butter

Whipped Cream

1 cup (235 ml) cold heavy cream

2 tbsp (16 g) confectioners' sugar

Maldon salt, for sprinkling

To make the caramel sauce, mix the heavy cream and vanilla in a medium-size saucepan, bring to a boil and set aside. In another medium-size saucepan, combine the corn syrup, granulated sugar, water and salt and bring to a boil. Cook the sugar mixture until it turns a light amber color and registers 300°F (150°C) on a thermometer clipped to the side of the pan. Remove it from the heat, CAREFULLY add a ladle of the hot cream and whisk. The cream and caramel mixture will boil up rapidly. Wait until it boils down before adding the rest of the cream. Whisk vigorously to dissolve all the caramelized sugar. Add the butter and carefully whisk to emulsify. Allow to cool, pour into a medium-size bowl and set aside. Caramel sauce can be made up to 2 weeks ahead and stored in an airtight container in the refrigerator.

To make the whipped cream, place the heavy cream and confectioners' sugar in the bowl of a stand mixer fitted with the whisk attachment and whip to medium peaks, 5 to 8 minutes. The peaks should hold their shape, but fall over slightly. Refrigerate the whipped cream until assembling the budino.

To assemble the budino, whisk the budino again until it's smooth. Spoon or pipe the budino into a glass serving dish. I like to use stemless wine glasses filled about one-third of the way with budino, but anything goes! Lightly tap the glass dish to level out the budino.

Drizzle the caramel sauce over the budino using a squeeze bottle or spoon to about ¼ inch (6 mm) thickness. Sprinkle the caramel layer with a pinch of Maldon salt. Dip a medium-size spoon into warm water and add a spoonful of whipped cream to the top of the budino. (Dipping the spoon into the water will allow the whipped cream to slide right off the spoon, giving it a rustic, natural look. You can also pipe the whipped cream on the top using a pastry bag fitted with a star tip for a more finished look.) Top the budino with a sprinkling of the toasted almonds. Serve.

> **Chef Tip:** Budino can be made a day ahead and stored in the refrigerator in an airtight container with plastic wrap covering the surface.

Lemon Meringue Bars with Raspberry Jam

Biting into a lemon bar is like biting into a summer day. This lemon bar is like that summer day dressed up for a night on the town. This bar will give you street cred. It's that cool. The two fundamentals of pastry at work here are a lemon curd and an Italian meringue. Master a curd and you're well on your way to learning a lemon meringue pie or a lemon soufflé. Master an Italian meringue and you're on your way to Italian meringue buttercream and even macarons. Here we're using a joconde, a sponge cake made from almond flour, for the base of the bar.

Makes 12 bars

Joconde Sponge Cake
¾ cup (90 g) confectioners' sugar

1 cup (120 g) almond flour

¼ cup (30 g) cake flour

1 tbsp (14 g) unsalted butter, at room temperature

3 eggs

3 egg whites (save the yolks for the curd)

Pinch of cream of tartar

2½ tbsp (30 g) granulated sugar

Raspberry Jam
6 tbsp (120 g) raspberry jam

2 tbsp (30 ml) water

To make the joconde, preheat the oven to 375°F (190°C). Lightly spray a sheet pan with cooking spray and lay parchment paper over it.

Sift the confectioners' sugar, almond flour and cake flour into the bowl of a stand mixer fitted with the paddle attachment. Add the butter and cream them together until combined, about 1 minute. Add the eggs one at a time, scraping down the sides and bottom of the bowl occasionally. The batter should be smooth and paste like. Transfer to a large bowl and set aside.

In the bowl of a stand mixer fitted with the whip attachment, whip the egg whites with the cream of tartar on medium speed until frothy, 1 to 2 minutes. Add the granulated sugar a little at a time and continue to whip to medium peaks, about 5 minutes. The meringue should hold its shape, but the tip of the peak will curl over onto itself when you lift the whisk attachment. (If the meringue becomes grainy, it is overwhipped. You might be able to save it by adding an additional egg white and mixing it into the meringue. However, your best bet is to start over with new egg whites.)

Fold half of the meringue into the batter until it is incorporated, followed by the second half. Pour the batter into the prepared sheet pan and level it out with an offset spatula. Try not to spread it too much to avoid deflating the batter.

Transfer the pan to the oven and bake the joconde for 12 to 15 minutes, until it's a pale golden just around the edges. Remove from the oven and set aside to cool.

To make the raspberry jam, place the raspberry jam and water in a small saucepan and cook over medium heat for 7 to 8 minutes to allow the jam to thicken. Remove it from the heat and set aside to cool.

Once the joconde cools, cut a 9 x 9–inch (23 x 23–cm) square from the center of the cake and evenly spread 3 tablespoons (60 g) of the raspberry jam on top. Line the inside of a straight-sided 9 x 9–inch (23 x 23–cm) baking pan with plastic wrap, overhanging the sides 1 to 2 inches (2.5 to 5 cm). Place the joconde square in the bottom of the pan, gently pressing it all the way down. Refrigerate the cake in the pan while making the curd.

(continued)

Lemon Curd
8 eggs

3 egg yolks

1¾ cups (350 g) granulated sugar

5 sheets silver leaf gelatin

9 tbsp (125 g) unsalted butter

1 cup (235 ml) freshly squeezed lemon juice

½ cup (50 g) lemon zest

Italian Meringue
5 egg whites

½ tsp cream of tartar

¾ cup (150 g) granulated sugar

⅓ cup (80 ml) water

To make the curd, in a large bowl, whisk together the eggs, egg yolks and granulated sugar until smooth and well combined. Place the gelatin in a small bowl and cover with cold water; set aside to let the gelatin bloom. Place the butter in a large bowl and set aside.

In a medium-size saucepan, combine the lemon juice and lemon zest and bring to a boil over medium heat. Temper the egg mixture by vigorously whisking the lemon juice mixture into it a little at a time to keep the eggs from curdling. Transfer the mixture back to the saucepan and boil it for 3 minutes, stirring constantly.

While the curd is boiling, drain the gelatin and place it in the bowl with the butter. Pour the hot curd over the butter and gelatin and blend with an immersion blender to emulsify the mixture. You can also place the mixture in a blender to emulsify it, stopping the blender occasionally to scrape down the sides. Once the curd is smooth, pour it over the joconde in the baking pan and lightly tap it on the counter to even out the curd. Place the pan in the refrigerator until set, 1 to 2 hours.

Once the bars are set, use the overhanging plastic wrap to lift the bars from the baking pan and cut them into twelve 2¼ x 3–inch (5.6 x 7.5–cm) bars (or your desired size). The lemon bars can be made 2 to 3 days ahead and refrigerated or frozen, wrapped in plastic in the pan.

To make the meringue, place the egg whites and cream of tartar in the bowl of a stand mixer fitted with the whisk attachment. Set aside. In a medium-size saucepan, combine the granulated sugar and water and cook over medium-high heat, stirring until the sugar dissolves. Use a pastry brush dipped in water to brush down the sides of the pan so all the sugar crystals dissolve. This will prevent the syrup from crystallizing and ruining your day. Continue to cook the syrup until it reaches 230°F (110°C) on a candy thermometer.

Begin to whip your egg whites and cream of tartar on medium speed while the simple syrup continues to cook. The goal here is to whip the egg whites to medium peaks about the same time as the syrup reaches soft-ball stage, 240°F (116°C). (The soft-ball stage is when a drop of sugar syrup placed in water forms a soft ball.) If they whip too fast, just keep them moving on low speed until the syrup catches up. Once the syrup reaches 240°F (116°C), turn the mixer to low speed and carefully pour the syrup in a slow stream down the side of the mixing bowl. Once it is added, turn the mixer to medium-high and whip it (whip it good) until the meringue is stiff and cooled.

Transfer the meringue to a piping bag fitted with the tip of your choice and pipe decoratively on the top of each lemon bar. Using a kitchen torch with a medium-high flame, gently toast the meringue. Serve!

Grasshopper Brownie Bars

Brownies are chewy, chocolaty rich treats by themselves. Making bar cookies is a good skill in itself, but when you start layering them with other pastry elements, the result is an impressive dessert that looks much more difficult to make than it actually is. We're pairing these brownies with a mint buttercream made with crème de menthe and a chocolate ganache glaze. However, you can layer this dessert with other spreadable goodies (think marshmallows)—it's up to you!

Makes 8 brownies

Brownies
Pan spray
1 cup (225 g) unsalted butter
6 oz (170 g) semisweet chocolate
2 large eggs
1⅓ cups (270 g) granulated sugar
2 tsp (10 ml) vanilla extract
1 tsp salt
1 cup (120 g) all-purpose flour

Mint Buttercream
10 tbsp (145 g) unsalted butter, at room temperature
3 tbsp (45 g) cream cheese, at room temperature
2¼ cups (270 g) confectioners' sugar
2 tbsp (30 ml) crème de menthe
1 tsp peppermint extract
⅛ tsp salt

Chocolate Ganache Glaze
6 oz (170 g) semisweet chocolate, chopped
¼ cup (60 ml) heavy cream
2 tbsp (28 g) unsalted butter

Chef Tip: Lightly sweep a kitchen torch set on a low flame across the chocolate ganache glaze to give it an extra shine before serving.

To make the brownies, preheat the oven to 350°F (180°C). Spray an 8 x 8–inch (20 x 20–cm) baking pan with cooking spray. Line the pan with a strip of parchment paper from one side to the other, with the parchment overhanging the pan on both sides by 1 to 2 inches (2.5 to 5 cm). Do this twice, so all sides of the pan are lined with parchment. You'll use parchment to pull the bars out of the pan later.

In a small saucepan, melt the butter over low heat until it's bubbling. Remove from the heat and add the chocolate. Stir the chocolate into the butter until it's melted and then set aside.

In the bowl of a stand mixer fitted with the whisk attachment, whisk the eggs, granulated sugar, vanilla and salt on medium speed until the eggs lighten in color and the mixture thickens, 2 to 3 minutes. Reduce the speed to low and add the chocolate/butter mixture. Remove the bowl from the stand mixer and fold in the flour by hand until just combined. Pour the batter into the parchment-lined pan and use an offset spatula to smooth the batter in an even layer.

Transfer to the oven and bake for 20 minutes, or until the brownies are set. A few moist crumbs should stick to a toothpick inserted into the center. Let the brownies cool completely, but do not refrigerate yet. The brownies can be made 2 days ahead and stored in the refrigerator, covered in the pan.

To make the buttercream, in the bowl of a stand mixer fitted with a paddle attachment, cream the butter and cream cheese on medium speed, until fully homogenized and smooth, 2 to 3 minutes. Reduce the speed to low and add the confectioners' sugar slowly, beating until smooth, 2 minutes. Finally, add the crème de menthe, peppermint extract and salt, and mix until fully incorporated. Gently press down on the cooled brownies to even out the tops. Using an offset spatula, smooth the buttercream in an even layer over the cooled brownies and refrigerate for at least 1 hour to allow the buttercream to harden.

To make the chocolate ganache glaze, melt the chocolate, heavy cream and butter in a heatproof bowl set over a pot of simmering water or in a double boiler, stirring until smooth. Pour the ganache glaze over the chilled buttercream brownies and tilt the pan to coat the top. Refrigerate the brownies for another hour, until all the layers are chilled and set. Remove the brownies from the pan, using the parchment paper to lift them. Slice the brownies into eight 2 x 4–inch (5 x 10–cm) bars (or your desired size). Wipe the knife between slices to keep the layers clean.

Strawberry–Balsamic Creamsicle Pops with Mint

Few things remind me of a being a child on a summer day like a creamsicle pop. Strawberry is always my hands-down favorite. For a cheffy twist, I incorporate balsamic vinegar and one of my favorite herbs—mint! Simple syrup is perfect to add sweetness to these pops and so many other dishes. Simple syrup is a technique with many uses, including Italian meringue, marshmallow and even sorbet!

Makes 10 creamsicles

Simple Syrup
1 cup (200 g) sugar
1 cup (235 ml) water

Strawberry Purée
½ cup (120 ml) heavy cream
4 cups (600 g) strawberries, hulled
30 mint leaves
2 tbsp (30 ml) freshly squeezed lemon juice
¼ cup (60 ml) balsamic vinegar

To make the simple syrup, combine the sugar and water in a small saucepan over medium-high heat. Stir the mixture until the sugar dissolves, bring it just to a boil and remove from the heat. Set aside to cool. You should have about 1¼ cups (295 ml) of simple syrup. Let the syrup cool completely.

To make the purée, mix the heavy cream and 6 tablespoons (90 ml) of the simple syrup in a small bowl. Set aside.

Cut 4 or 5 strawberries into ¼-inch (6-mm) slices and reserve for garnish. Purée the rest of the strawberries and the mint leaves in a blender. Add ¾ cup (180 ml) of the simple syrup and the lemon juice to the strawberry purée and blend again. Taste the mixture for flavor balance. If the strawberries taste on the acidic side and lack sugar, add more of the simple syrup to balance them out. You can also add more mint to your taste. Add the balsamic vinegar to the purée in two parts, tasting again for flavor balance. The vinegar should complement the strawberries and not overpower them.

Using a liquid measuring cup or other small container with a spout, pour the strawberry mixture into 3-ounce (84-g) popsicle molds, leaving 1 inch (2.5 cm) of space at the top. Slide the strawberry slices down the inside of the molds, right onto the plastic surface, trying not to leave any space between the strawberry slice and the mold. Pour a splash of the reserved heavy cream/simple syrup mixture into each mold toward the sides, until each one is almost filled. Leave a small space for expansion when you insert the popsicle stick. Insert the popsicle sticks and freeze the pops until solid, 4 to 5 hours.

Variation: Strawberry–Balsamic Creamsicle Pops with Basil
Substitute 20 basil leaves for the mint leaves.

Chef Tip: Taste the pop base before you freeze. Fruit varies in sugar levels based on ripeness. Freezing mutes flavors. If the base is lacking sweetness, add a bit more syrup.

Sweet and Salty Brown Butter Chocolate Chip Cookies

Cookies are always a crowd-pleaser. They come in an infinite array of flavors and textures and are sure to put a smile on your guests' faces. Chocolate chip cookies are a classic drop cookie (cookies dropped onto the pan from a spoon or scoop and then baked). These golden, rich, buttery cookies have the sweet contrast of chocolate chips. Everyone should know how to make them. We're changing up the original recipe here by browning the butter to give it an added level of rich, nutty flavor, then topping it with a little garnish of salt. We recommend using fleur de sel, but any salt will do in a pinch.

Makes 18 large cookies

3 cups (360 g) all-purpose flour

1 tsp baking soda

1 tsp kosher salt

1 cup (225 g) unsalted butter

½ cup (112 g) firmly packed light brown sugar

½ cup (112 g) firmly packed dark brown sugar

½ cup (100 g) granulated sugar

2 large eggs, lightly beaten

2 tsp (10 ml) vanilla extract

1¾ cups (305 g) good-quality semisweet chocolate chips (I like Guittard)

Fleur de sel, for garnish

Line two baking sheets with parchment paper or silicone baking mats.

Whisk the flour, baking soda and salt in a medium-size bowl.

Melt the butter in a medium-size saucepan over medium heat. (Note: Using a light-colored pan will help you see the color of the butter as it browns.) The butter will begin to foam. Stir the butter consistently and cook until it is a dark amber color (darker browned butter is better for baked goods), about 6 minutes. Transfer the butter immediately to a separate bowl to prevent burning. Let it cool for 15 minutes.

In a large bowl, combine all the sugars, eggs, vanilla and browned butter. Add the flour mixture in two parts and mix until just combined. Do not overmix your dough. Fold the chocolate chips in gently.

Scoop the dough with an ice cream scoop, large cookie scoop or large spoon and drop onto the prepared baking sheet 2 inches (5 cm) apart. Press down on the cookies lightly to flatten them a little bit. Refrigerate the dough for 1 hour on the cookie sheets. (Chilling the cookie dough before baking helps the cookies retain their shape when baked—no more flat cookies.) You can also freeze the dough at this point and pull it out whenever you want cookies! Freeze it in an airtight container and allow it to thaw on the cookie sheets for 15 minutes before baking.

Preheat the oven to 350°F (180°C).

Remove the baking sheets from the refrigerator and sprinkle the cookies lightly with fleur de sel. Bake for 12 to 15 minutes, until just cooked through and slightly golden. Allow them to cool for 5 minutes on the baking sheets, then transfer to a wire rack to cool.

> **Chef Tip:** You can store the dough as a log. Wrap the finished dough with plastic and roll it into a 5-inch (12.5-cm) log. Chill until ready to use. You can cut slices off the dough and bake.

Stone Fruit Crumble with Blackberries

Don't underestimate how delicious this simple dessert is. With its tender, sweet, crumbly texture, a crumble is an excellent way to showcase seasonal fruit. The key technique here is making a streusel. Streusel is that delicious crumb topping on muffins, coffee cakes and pies. It can be made, baked and used to top anything you want. Most streusels are made with flour, sugar and butter. I love this version, which incorporates almonds. Feel free to swap out the almonds with more flour if you have a nut allergy. You can substitute your favorite fruits in this recipe as well as add different spice profiles to the crumble itself (such as cinnamon).

Serves 6-8

1 lb (454 g) peaches, pitted and cut into ½" (1.3-cm) cubes

1 lb (454 g) nectarines, pitted and cut into ½" (1.3-cm) cubes

6 oz (168 g) fresh blackberries, picked through and rinsed

1 cup (120 g) all-purpose flour

¾ cup (85 g) sliced almonds

1 cup (200 g) sugar

½ tsp salt

10 tbsp (140 g) unsalted butter, cut into ½" (1.3-cm) cubes and refrigerated

Burnt Milk Ice Cream (page 180) or Vanilla Ice Cream (page 180), for serving

Preheat the oven to 425°F (220°C).

Place the peaches and nectarines in the bottom of a 9-inch (23-cm) pie dish or an 8-inch (20-cm) square glass baking dish. Sprinkle the blackberries evenly on top of the stone fruit. Set the dish aside.

Combine the flour, sliced almonds, sugar and salt in the bowl of a food processor. Process them until the almonds are roughly ground. Add the cold butter to the processor bowl and pulse until the mixture just begins to come together. It should look sandy with some clumps and should hold together when you squeeze it in your hand. If it is all sticking together, you've gone a little too far, but it will still taste good, so I say use it!

Using your hands, sprinkle the mixture on top of the fruit in the pie dish, covering all the fruit. Bake the crisp on the lower rack of the oven (use the middle rack for more browning) for 25 to 30 minutes, until the topping is golden. Serve with ice cream.

Variations
Cook seasonally with your fruit. Here are some of my favorites.
Winter: Apples and cranberries
Spring: Rhubarb and strawberries
Summer: Berries and stone fruit
Fall: Pears and persimmon

Chef Tip: Taste and adjust! If the fruit is tart and lacks sweetness, add 1 tablespoon (12 g) of sugar at a time to the fruit mix until balanced. Some fruits are sweet and lack acid, so adding lemon juice will brighten up any crisp.

Date Bread Pudding with Almonds

Custards (basically heated milk/cream, eggs and sugar) serve as the base for myriad desserts. Custards can be stirred on the stovetop (crème anglaise, pastry cream, puddings) or baked or steamed (flan, crème brûlée, bread pudding). It's hard to believe this rich, custard-soaked comfort food originated as a frugal way to use stale bread. You can substitute different types of bread, such as croissants or cinnamon rolls—heck, even doughnuts—for the brioche in this recipe.

Serves 8

Softened butter, for the pan

1 lb (454 g) brioche loaf, cut into 1" (2.5-cm) cubes

2 cups (360 g) pitted dates, chopped

½ cup (60 g) sliced almonds

8 large eggs

1 cup (235 ml) heavy cream

3 cups (705 ml) whole milk

1¼ cups (250 g) granulated sugar

1 tbsp (15 ml) vanilla extract

¼ tsp ground nutmeg

Confectioners' sugar, for garnish

Vanilla Ice Cream (page 180), for serving

Butter a 9 x 13–inch (23 x 33–cm) glass baking dish.

In a large bowl, toss the brioche cubes with the dates, then line the bottom of the baking dish with the bread mixture. Sprinkle the almonds over the top.

Make the custard using the same large bowl (why wash an extra dish?). Whisk together the eggs, heavy cream, whole milk, granulated sugar, vanilla and nutmeg until thoroughly combined. Pour the custard over the brioche mixture in the baking dish. Let the mixture stand for 30 minutes, lightly pressing on the bread cubes occasionally to fully submerge them in the custard.

Preheat the oven to 350°F (180°C).

Bake the bread pudding for 45 minutes, or until the center is just set. The pudding should still have a slight jiggle to it, but be cooked through. Sprinkle with the confectioners' sugar and serve with a scoop of vanilla ice cream.

> **Chef Tip:** Some of our favorite additions to this bread pudding are raisins, chocolate chips, white chocolate chips and nuts. Sprinkle in while the bread is soaking in the custard.

Vanilla Soufflé with Fresh Berries and Whipped Cream

Soufflés are made from a French meringue base. Whipping sugar in egg whites gives them the structure to puff up into sweet clouds. I use a béchamel base for this vanilla soufflé; it's a rich white sauce made from a roux with the addition of milk. Coating the ramekins with butter and sugar creates a hint of a caramelized sugary crust along the sides.

Makes 6 soufflés

½ cup (112 g) unsalted butter, plus more for the ramekins

⅔ cup (125 g) granulated sugar, plus more for the ramekins

6 eggs, separated

½ cup (60 g) all-purpose flour

1½ cups (355 ml) cold whole milk

1 tbsp (15 g) vanilla bean paste or (15 ml) vanilla extract

½ tsp cream of tartar

For Garnish

Confectioners' sugar

Fresh berries

Whipped Cream (page 188)

Variation: Chocolate Soufflé

Melt the ½ cup (112 g) of butter with 8 ounces (224 g) of good-quality chocolate (about 62% cacao) and omit the flour and milk. Follow the directions beginning with whisking the egg yolks into the melted chocolate.

Preheat the oven to 375°F (190°C). Butter the inside of six 6-ounce (168-g) ramekins all the way up the sides to the top edge. Coat them with sugar and pour out any excess sugar. Refrigerate on a sheet pan while you prepare the soufflés.

Place the egg yolks in a large bowl and set aside.

In a medium-size saucepan over medium heat, melt the butter. Whisk in the flour and cook, whisking constantly, for about 30 seconds. Add the cold milk and vanilla bean paste to the pan. Bring the béchamel to a boil while whisking, making sure to whisk away any lumps. (Note: Adding cold milk to a hot roux prevents lumps.) Remove the pan from the heat and temper the egg yolks into the mixture. Add about a ladle of the béchamel to the egg yolks and whisk vigorously. Repeat the process until the yolks are fully incorporated into the béchamel sauce. Place plastic wrap over the top of the béchamel so a skin does not form and allow it to cool to warm.

In the bowl of a stand mixer fitted with the whisk attachment, whip the egg whites and the cream of tartar on medium-high speed until frothy, about 2 minutes. Slowly pour the granulated sugar into the whites while they whip, about 1 tablespoon (12 g) at a time. Whip the whites until they're stiff yet still glossy, not dry, about 5 minutes.

Whisk one-quarter of the meringue into the béchamel sauce to loosen it. Fold the rest of the meringue into the béchamel in two parts until just combined. Fold gently so the meringue doesn't deflate and prevent the soufflés from rising. (Note: Always fold lighter ingredients into heavier ingredients.) Fill the ramekins to the rim with the soufflé batter and bake them on the sheet pan in the lower third of the oven for 15 to 17 minutes, until the soufflés are golden at the edges and rise 1 to 1½ inches (2.5 to 3.8 cm) above the rim of the ramekin. Never open the oven while the soufflés are baking.

Sprinkle the confectioners' sugar over the top of the soufflés and serve with the fresh berries and whipped cream.

ACKNOWLEDGMENTS

To our parents, Kathie McKee, Walt and Karen McKee, Mary Tila and Pat Tila for endless support and encouragement. Thanks for always showing us how to work hard and chase our dreams.

Bobby Flay! We know you've written only a handful of forewords in 30 years. We are honored to call you our friend and mentor. You've taught us how to believe in ourselves and fight for what's important in food and business.

Alton Brown, for your unending support and mentorship: there would be no books without you.

Chef Neal Fraser, for opening his kitchen to both of us and being a teacher and a mentor. Thank you for giving us our first restaurant jobs, be it twenty years apart.

Chefs Jim Dodge and Sherry Yard, for recipe inspiration, guidance and teaching us that you can be the best and humble at the same time.

Jose Gordillo, pastry superstar and Ali's right-hand man. We couldn't have done it without your organization, eye for detail, unparalleled work ethic, kitchen ninja skills and good sense of humor.

Danielle Zecca, for your skill and eye for detail refining our recipes.

The photo team of Ken Goodman, Joann Cianculli and Sophia Green, for making the photos delicious.

Cecilia De Castro, for being a skilled, patient culinary instructor and giving Ali the foundation for her pastry passion.

Sarah Monroe, William Kiester and the team at Page Street, for always believing in us and teaching us chefs how to write great cookbooks.

To the entire pastry team at Red Bird restaurant: Chef Kasra "It's Gonna Be Great" Ajdari, Chef Tessa Rose Schwartz, Luis Becerra, Eric Cowger and all the friendly chefs and kitchen crew, for being incredibly generous with their time and teaching. And for answering endless culinary questions from Ali! You guys are absolutely the best.

To Team Tila: Taji Marie, Joanna Mendoza, Meagan Van Deren and Sierra Scott, for the inspiration and making sure the Tila machine is always running smoothly.

Last but never least, our fans! There would be no us without your love, support and feedback! We are forever grateful for you!

ABOUT THE AUTHORS

Jet Tila is a chef, culinary anthropologist, entrepreneur and Food Network star. He was born into the first Thai food family of Los Angeles, California, a family that established the first Thai markets and restaurants in the United States.

As the inaugural Culinary Ambassador of Thai Cuisine, a title and role entrusted to him by the Royal Thai Consul-General, Jet appears far and wide. He has made notable appearances on *Iron Chef America, Parts Unknown, Chopped, Cutthroat Kitchen, Beat Bobby Flay, Guy's Grocery Games* and the *Today* show. Jet has recieved a Dream of Los Angeles Award, a distinction given out annually by the Mayor of Los Angeles.

Jet also partnered with the Wynn Resorts to open Wazuzu, a groundbreaking take on Pan-Asian dining, at the Encore Casino and Resort on the Las Vegas Strip. He has inspired and cultivated a concept in partnership with the largest food service company in the world, Compass Group. Along with his education at Le Cordon Bleu, Jet also completed an intensive study program at the California Sushi Academy. Predominantly cooking Thai and Chinese cuisines, Jet showcases an overall cooking style that represents the neighborhood he grew up in L.A.

Jet is the author of the bestselling cookbook *101 Asian Dishes You Need to Cook Before You Die.* From a kid growing up in L.A. in a Thai and Chinese family to a prominent chef and restaurant owner, Jet has written this book as both a chronology of culinary tradition and its rediscovery. *101 Epic Dishes* is his second book.

Ali Tila is a pastry chef and lifestyle expert. She attended pastry school in Los Angeles and currently works at Red Bird restaurant. As Jet's wife and business partner, she co-owns and manages the Team Tila culinary empire. Ali's instructional culinary videos and live-streamed interactive videos on Facebook have hundreds of thousands of views. Her skills in the kitchen are very well rounded, ranging from baking and pastry to how to make the perfect steak. She created the very popular live-streamed segment #EatLikeaPro with Jet that teaches people how to navigate ethnic restaurants, ordering and eating like a pro. She creates family, kids and lifestyle content and regularly contributes to and manages her own and Jet's social media portfolios. She and Jet have two children.

INDEX